Passport to Advanced Mathematics Test 2

"You never fail until you stop trying" - Albert Einstein

For inquiries;
info@xmprep.com

Passport to Advanced Mathematics
Test 2 #2

Test Taking Tips

- ☐ Take a deep breath and relax
- ☐ Read directions carefully
- ☐ Read the questions thoroughly
- ☐ Make sure you understand what is being asked
- ☐ Go over all of the choices before you answer
- ☐ Paraphrase the question
- ☐ Eliminate the options you know are wrong
- ☐ Check your work
- ☐ Think positively and do your best

Table of Contents

Math Test – Calculator

DIRECTIONS

For multiple choice questions, choose the best answers from the choices after you solve the questions. Check your answers from the answer key.

For free responce questions, find your answer, write it in the space provided below and finally check it from the answer key.

NOTES

1. Calculator **is allowed**.
2. All variables are real numbers unless otherwise indicated.
3. Figures of this test are drawn to scale unless otherwise indicated.
4. Figures of this test lie in a plane.
5. Unless otherwise stated, the domain of function *f* is the set of all real numbers *x* for which *f*(*x*) is a real number.

REFERENCE

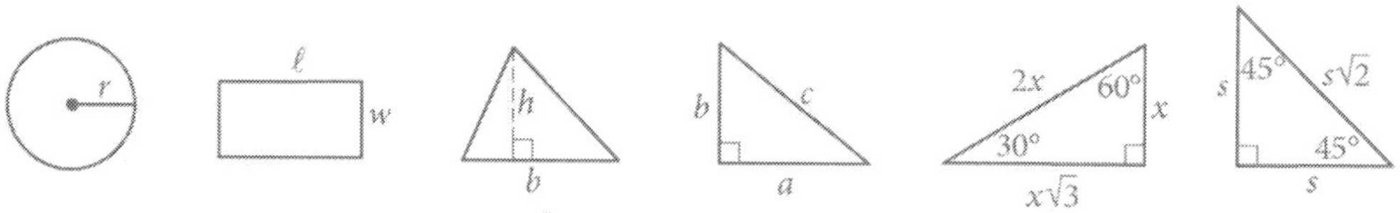

$A = \pi r^2$ $C = 2\pi r$ | $A = \ell w$ | $A = \frac{1}{2}bh$ | $c^2 = a^2 + b^2$ | Special Right Triangles

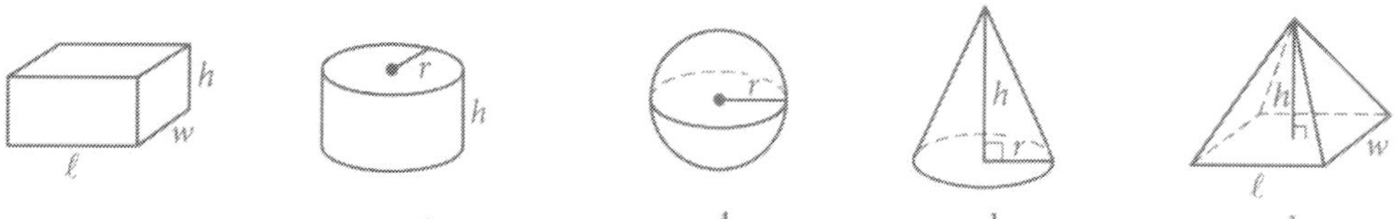

$V = \ell wh$ | $V = \pi r^2 h$ | $V = \frac{4}{3}\pi r^3$ | $V = \frac{1}{3}\pi r^2 h$ | $V = \frac{1}{3}\ell wh$

The number of degrees of a circle is 360.

The number of radians of a circle is 2π.

The sum of the angles of a triangle is 180 degrees.

CONTINUE ▶

1

$$P(x) = 3x^3 - 2x^2 - 12x + 8$$

What is the sum of the roots of the polynomial given above?

A) 0
B) 0.66
C) 1.5
D) 4.66

2

$$\frac{8x^6 + 16x^4 - 24x^3}{4x^2}$$

Which of the following is equivalent to the expression above?

A) $8x^2 + 4x - 6$
B) $2x^4 + 4x^2 - 6$
C) $2x^4 + 4x^2 - 6x$
D) $8x^6 + 4x^4 - 6x$

3

$$\frac{10x^2 + x - 21}{2x + 3}$$

If $ax + b$ represents the simplified form of the expression, then what is the value of $a + b$?

A) -12
B) -2
C) 2
D) 7

4

$$x^7 + Mx^3 - 2x + 3$$

Find the value of M if $(x-1)$ is a factor of the polynomial given above.

A) -2
B) 0
C) 1
D) 2

5

$$P(x) = mx^2 + 2nx + 7$$

If $P(-2) = P(1)$, what is the value of $m - 2n$?

A) -2
B) -1
C) 0
D) 2

6

$$Q(x) = 5(x^2 + 7x + 4) + 2(x - n)$$

The polynomial $Q(x)$ is defined above. If $Q(x)$ is divisible by x, what is the value of n?

A) -10
B) -2
C) 0
D) 10

CONTINUE ▶

7

$$y = ax^3 + bx + c$$

The polynomial given above passes through the point (-1,1). Which of the following must be true?

A) $a - b = -1$
B) $-b + c = -1 + a$
C) $a + b - c = -1$
D) $a - b - c = 1$

8

$$P(x) = x^2 + 4x + 11 \qquad P(\sqrt{7} - 2) = Q$$

What is the value of Q?

A) 12
B) 14
C) 22
D) 30

9

$$P(x, y) = 2xy^2 - 3x^2y + 4x - 5y + 2x^3y$$

What is the value of $P(-1, 2)$?

A) -32
B) -18
C) -16
D) 12

10

$$2(5k + 4)(3k + 2)(3k) = 0$$

How many different possible values of k satisfy the equation given above?

A) One
B) Two
C) Three
D) Four

11

If $x^2 - 2x + 3 = m$ and $-2x + 7 = n$, which of the following is the sum of the roots of $m + n$?

A) -4
B) -2
C) 4
D) 10

12

$$5x^{11} + 3x^8 - A$$

When the polynomial given above is divided by $x + 1$, the remainder is 17. What is the remainder if the polynomial above is divided by $x - 1$?

A) -19
B) -11
C) 27
D) 34

13

$$x^2 + 6x + 15 = (x - 2)(x + 8) + m$$

Based on the polynomial equality given above, what is the value of *m*?

A) -1
B) 15
C) 16
D) 31

14

$$-2x^2 + 4x - 7$$

If the polynomial given above is multiplied by 3*x* - 5, what is the coefficient of *x* in the resulting polynomial?

A) -41
B) -8
C) -1
D) 1

15

$$x^3 + mx + n = (x^2 + 1)Q(x) + 3x - 2$$

According to the polynomial equation given above, what is the value of *m* + *n*?

A) 2
B) 4
C) 6
D) 8

16

$$P(x) = 7x^4 - 3x^3 + 5x + 3$$
$$Q(x) = -4x^4 - 2x^3 - x^2 - 3x + 4$$

Polynomials $P(x)$ and $Q(x)$ are given above. Find the polynomial $2P(x) - 3Q(x)$.

A) $26x^4 + 3x^2 + 19x - 6$
B) $26x^4 + 3x^2 + 13x + 18$
C) $13x^4 - 4x^3 - 2x^2 - 6x + 17$
D) $2x^4 - 12x^3 - 3x^2 + x - 6$

17

$$\frac{(x+y)^2 + (x-y)^2}{x^2 + y^2}$$

What is the simplified form of the equation above?

A) 1
B) 2
C) x
D) xy

18

$$P(x) = (a-2)x^3 - (b+1)x^2 - 2x + 4$$
$$Q(x) = 5x^3 + 2x^2 - cx + d - 3$$

The polynomials *P*(*x*) and *Q*(*x*) are given above. If the polynomials are equal, then what is the value of *a* + *b* + *c* + *d*?

A) 7
B) 8
C) 11
D) 13

19

If $h(x-2)=5x^2+3x-9$, then which of the following defines $h(x)$?

A) $5x^2+3x-7$
B) $5x^2+3x-11$
C) $5x^2+23x+17$
D) $5x^2+23x+23$

20

$$P(x) = ax^4 + bx^2 + c$$

The polynomial $P(x)$ is defined above. If $P(1)$ is equal to -12, what is the value of $P(-1)$?

A) -12
B) 12
C) 0
D) It can not be determined.

21

$$(x-2)P(x)=3x^2-mx+3m+2$$

Given the polynomial above, what is the value of $P(1)$?

A) -20
B) -16
C) 23
D) 33

22

$$P(x)=2x^2 \quad Q(x)=4x^3$$

$$P(3x^5)\cdot Q(2x^4)=m\cdot x^n$$

Given the operations with polynomials above, what is the value of $m+n$?

A) 70
B) 576
C) 590
D) 598

23

$$3x^2 - 4y^2 = 11$$

$$x^2 + y^2 = 13$$

If $x > 0$ and $y > 0$ in the equations given above, what is the value of $x^y + y^x$?

A) 6
B) 12
C) 17
D) 18

24

$$(x-a)^2 = x^2 - 6x + b$$

Based on the equation given above, what is the value of $a+b$?

A) 3
B) 6
C) 9
D) 12

25

If $x^2 + mx + n = (x - 2)(x + 6)$, what is the value of mn?

A) -48
B) -12
C) 4
D) 24

26

$$P(x) = ax^2 + bx + c$$

The polynomial $P(x)$ is defined above. If $P(1)$ is equal to $P(-1)$, what is the value of b?

A) -1
B) 1
C) 0
D) It can not be determined.

27

$$P(ax) = x^4 - 2x^3 + x + b$$

If $P(-2a) = 44$, then what is the value of b?

A) 10
B) 14
C) 42
D) 46

28

$$P(x+2y, x-3y) = y^2 + 2x - m$$

What is the value of m if P(7,-3) is equal to 8?

A) 0
B) 1
C) 2
D) 5

29

$$P(x) = (3x^3 - 4x^2 + x - 5)\cdot(2x^2 - 5x + 1)$$
$$P(x) = ax^5 + bx^4 + cx^3 + dx^2 + ex + f$$

Given the polynomial $P(x)$ above, what is the value of $b + c$?

A) 2
B) 23
C) 25
D) 48

30

$$x^2 + 4x + c = 0$$

If the equation above has two distinct real solutions, which of the following can not be the value of c?

A) -1
B) 1
C) 3
D) 5

CONTINUE ▶

31

$$P(x) = x^3 - (m+1)x^2 + (n+1)x + k - 5$$
$$Q(x) = (x^2 - 3)(x+1)$$

If the polynomilas $P(x)$ and $Q(x)$ are equal, then what is the value of $\frac{m-n}{k}$?

A) 1
B) 2
C) 3
D) 4

32

$$x^2 + ax - 5 = (x+1)(bx+c)$$

In the equation above **x** is a real number. What is the value of **a** +**b** +**c**?

A) -8
B) -5
C) 1
D) 9

33

$$P(x) = x^3 + 4x^2 + 2mx - 5$$

When the polynomial given above is divided by (*x*-1) the remainder is 4. What will be the remainder when the polynomial is divided by (*x*-2)?

A) 11
B) 27
C) 32
D) 37

34

$(4x^2 - \frac{3}{2}x + 5)$ is multiplied by $(8x + \frac{1}{4})$. What is the coefficient of x^2?

A) −11
B) 1
C) 12
D) 32

35

$$P(x+2y, x-3y) = y^2 + 3x - 5$$

According to the polynomial equation given above, what is the value of P(7,2)?

A) 6
B) 7
C) 9
D) 11

36

$$(a^2b - 2b^2 + 5ab^2) - (-a^2b + 8ab^2 + 3b^2)$$

Which of the following is equivalent to the expression above?

A) $b^2 + 13ab^2$
B) $2a^2b + b^2 - 3a^2b$
C) $-3a^2b - 5b^2$
D) $2a^2b - 3ab^2 - 5b^2$

CONTINUE ▶

37

$$P(x) = 3x^3 + 4x$$
$$Q(x) = -2x^4 + x^3 + x^2$$

Polynomials $P(x)$ and $Q(x)$ are given above. Find the polynomial $P(x^2) + Q(x)$.

A) $3x^6 + 4x^5 - 2x^4$
B) $3x^5 + 4x^4 + 2x^3$
C) $3x^6 - 2x^4 + x^3 + 5x^2$
D) $-2x^4 + 4x^3 + x^2 + 4x$

38

$$a^2 + 16 - 2a = 6a$$

What is the value of $2a - 1$ based on the equation given above?

A) 7
B) 9
C) 11
D) 17

39

$$x^2 + ax - 5 = (x+1)(bx+c)$$

According to the polynomial equation given above, what is the value of $a + b + c$?

A) -9
B) -8
C) 0
D) 8

40

$$P(x) = x^2 + x - 4 \qquad Q(x) = -2x^2 - 5x + 1$$
$$n \cdot P(-2) = Q(-2)$$

Based on the polynomial equations given above, what is the value of n?

A) -0.5
B) 1
C) -1.5
D) 2

41

When polynomial $P(x)$ is divided by $(x + 2)$, the remainder is 3. Which of the following must be true about $P(x)$?

A) $P(2) = 3$
B) $P(3) = 2$
C) $P(-2) = 3$
D) $P(-3) = -2$

42

If $a = 3x^2 - x + 2$, $b = x^2 + 5$, $c = 4x - 7$, then find $2a - (3b + c)$?

A) $2x^2 - 5x - 10$
B) $3x^2 + 2x - 18$
C) $3x^2 - 6x - 4$
D) $9x^2 + 2x + 12$

43

$$P(x) = ax + b$$

$$P(2x + 1) + P(3x - 1) = 5x + 6$$

What is the value of $P(0)$?

A) -2
B) -1
C) 3
D) 6

44

$$144x^2 - 36 = a^2(bx - c)(bx + c)$$

If a, b, and c are positive integers, which of the following can be the value of $a + b + c$?

A) 9
B) 11
C) 19
D) All of the above

45

$$2x - 4 = ax(x-1) + bx(x+1) + c(x^2 - 1)$$

What is the value of $a \cdot b \cdot c$?

A) 6
B) 8
C) 10
D) 12

46

If $x^2 = 4$ and $y^2 = 9$, which of the following is a possible value of $(x + 4y)^2$?

A) 40
B) 100
C) 144
D) 148

47

$$a^2 - b^2 - a + b$$

If one of the factors of the expression above is $a - b$, then what is the other factor of it?

A) $a + b - 1$
B) $a + b + 1$
C) $a - b + 1$
D) $-a + 2b + 1$

48

$$\frac{a^8 + 4a^2 - 8}{a^2 + 2}$$

What is the result of the operation given above?

A) $a^6 + 4a^2 - 4$
B) $a^6 - a^5 - 4$
C) $a^6 - 2a^4 + 4a^2 - 4$
D) $a^6 - a^5 + 4a^4 - 4$

49

If $p(x) = ax^2 + bx + c$ and $p(1) = 8$, $p(-1) = 6$ then find $a + c$.

A) 2
B) 7
C) 14
D) 48

50

$$P(x) = x^2 - 2x + 5 \qquad Q(x) = x^3 - 5x + 2$$

$$R(x) = 3P(4x^3) + 4Q(5x^4)$$

The polynomial $R(x)$ is defined in terms of polynomials $P(x)$ and $Q(x)$. What is the constant term of $R(x)$?

A) 7
B) 23
C) 30
D) 100

51

$$h(x) = ax^2 + bx + c$$

If $h(0) = 7$, $h(1) = 19$, and $h(-1) = 13$, then what is the value of $a + b + c$?

A) 3
B) 7
C) 9
D) 19

52

$$(-x^2 + 3x + 7)(6x^5 - 3x^4 + x^2 + 2x - 5)$$

After the multiplication of the polynomials given above, what will be the coefficient of the x^3 term?

A) -2
B) 1
C) 3
D) 5

53

$$p(x) = 2(3x^2 + 12x + 15) - 6(x - m)$$

The polynomial $p(x)$ is defined above. If m is a constant and $p(x)$ is divisible by x, then what is the value of m?

A) -3
B) -2.5
C) -5
D) 5

54

$$a + b = 4$$

$$b - c = 3$$

What is the value of $ab - ac + b^2 - bc$?

A) 4
B) 8
C) 12
D) 16

CONTINUE ▶

55

$$P(x) = x^4 + \frac{1}{2}x^3 + x^2 + ax$$

If the polynomial given above is divisible by $x^2 + 1$, then what is the value of a?

A) $-\frac{1}{3}$
B) $-\frac{1}{2}$
C) $\frac{1}{2}$
D) $\frac{1}{3}$

56

$$\frac{x^2 + ax + b}{x^2 + 11x + 28} \cdot \frac{x^2 + 4x - 21}{x^2 - 9} = \frac{x+2}{x+3}$$

What is the value of $a + b$?

A) 10
B) 12
C) 14
D) 16

57

$$x(x-4)(x+6)(x-2)$$

Which of the following is the equivalent to the polynomial above?

A) $x^4 + 12x^3$
B) $x^3 - 4x^2 + 4x - 48$
C) $x^4 - 4x^3 + 4x^2 - 48x$
D) $x^4 - 28x^2 + 48x$

58

$$x^2 - 4y = -7$$
$$y^2 - 2x = 2$$

What is the value of $x + y$?

A) 3
B) 4
C) 5
D) 7

59

$$A = a + b + c$$
$$B = a - b - c$$

Given the equations above find the value of $A^2 - B^2$.

A) $4a(b+c)$
B) $4b(a+c)$
C) $2c(a+b)$
D) $2a(b-c)$

60

$$P(x) = x^3 + 24$$

What is the remainder when the polynomial given above is divided by $x - 2$?

CONTINUE ▶

61

What real value of x makes the equation $x^3 - 5x^2 + 2x - 10 = 0$ true?

62

Alexis has finished weaving a blanket. She made the blanket length four feet greater than twice its width.

If the area covered by the blanket is 70 square feet, how many feet is the length longer than the width of the blanket?

63

$$P(x) = 5x^2 - (a+3)x + 14$$
$$Q(x) = (b+2)x^2 - 2x + c + 9$$

If polynomial $P(x)$ is equal to the polynomial $Q(x)$, then what is the value of $a+b+c$?

64

$$\frac{2x+1}{x^2-5x+6} = \frac{A}{x-3} + \frac{B}{x-2}$$

Based on the expression given above what is the value of A - B?

65

$$3x^4 + 8x^3 + 12x^2 + 5x - m$$

For what value of m is the polynomial above divisible by $x + 2$?

66

If $a+b = 4$ and c-$d = 6$, then what is the value of $3(bc\text{-}ad\text{-}bd+ac)$?

CONTINUE ▶

67

$$Q(x) = ax^2 + bx + c$$
$$Q(x-1) = (x-4)^2$$

Based on the polynomials given above find the value of $a+b+c$?

68

$$P(x) = 3x^2 - 5x - 7 + c$$

If $P(1.5) = 19$ in the polynomial given above, then what is the value of $P(-0.5)$?

SECTION 1 - OPERATIONS WITH POLYNOMIALS

#	Answer	Topic	Subtopic	#	Answer	Topic	Subtopic	#	Answer	Topic	Subtopic	#	Answer	Topic	Subtopic
1	B	TB	S8	18	D	TB	S8	35	D	TB	S8	52	B	TB	S8
2	C	TB	S8	19	C	TB	S8	36	D	TB	S8	53	C	TB	S8
3	B	TB	S8	20	A	TB	S8	37	C	TB	S8	54	C	TB	S8
4	A	TB	S8	21	C	TB	S8	38	A	TB	S8	55	C	TB	S8
5	C	TB	S8	22	D	TB	S8	39	B	TB	S8	56	C	TB	S8
6	D	TB	S8	23	C	TB	S8	40	C	TB	S8	57	D	TB	S8
7	C	TB	S8	24	D	TB	S8	41	C	TB	S8	58	A	TB	S8
8	B	TB	S8	25	A	TB	S8	42	C	TB	S8	59	A	TB	S8
9	A	TB	S8	26	C	TB	S8	43	C	TB	S8	60	32	TB	S8
10	C	TB	S8	27	B	TB	S8	44	D	TB	S8	61	5	TB	S8
11	C	TB	S8	28	C	TB	S8	45	D	TB	S8	62	9	TB	S8
12	C	TB	S8	29	A	TB	S8	46	B	TB	S8	63	7	TB	S8
13	D	TB	S8	30	D	TB	S8	47	A	TB	S8	64	12	TB	S8
14	A	TB	S8	31	A	TB	S8	48	C	TB	S8	65	22	TB	S8
15	A	TB	S8	32	A	TB	S8	49	B	TB	S8	66	72	TB	S8
16	A	TB	S8	33	B	TB	S8	50	B	TB	S8	67	4	TB	S8
17	B	TB	S8	34	A	TB	S8	51	D	TB	S8	68	23	TB	S8

Topics & Subtopics

Code	Description
SB8	Operations with Polynomials

Code	Description
TB	Passport to Advanced Mathematics

CONTINUE ▶

1

$$P(x) = 3x^3 - 2x^2 - 12x + 8$$

$P(x) = x^2(3x-2) - 4(3x-2)$

What is the sum of the roots of the polynomial given above?

$P(x) = (3x-2) \cdot (x^2-4)$

A) 0 $P(x) = (3x-2) \cdot (x-2)(x+2)$

B) 0.66 $3x-2=0$ $x=2$ $x=-2$
                  $+2$ $+2$

C) 1.5 $\dfrac{3x}{3} = \dfrac{2}{3}$ $x = 0.66$

D) 4.66 $2-2+0.66 = 0.66$

2

$$\frac{8x^6 + 16x^4 - 24x^3}{4x^2}$$

Which of the following is equivalent to the expression above?

$\dfrac{8x^6}{4x^2} + \dfrac{16x^4}{4x^2} - \dfrac{24x^3}{4x^2}$

A) $8x^2 + 4x - 6$

B) $2x^4 + 4x^2 - 6$

C) $2x^4 + 4x^2 - 6x$ $2x^4 + 4x^2 - 6x$

D) $8x^6 + 4x^4 - 6x$

3

$$\frac{10x^2 + x - 21}{2x + 3}$$

If $ax + b$ represents the simplified form of the expression, then what is the value of $a + b$?

A) -12

B) -2

C) 2

D) 7

$5x - 7$ $ax + b$

$2x+3 \overline{) 10x^2 + x - 21}$ $a = 5$

$+ \underline{-10x^2 \mp 15x}$ $+ b = -7$

       $-14x - 21$ $a + b = -2$

     $+ \underline{+ 14x + 21}$

           0

4

$$x^7 + Mx^3 - 2x + 3$$

Find the value of M if $(x-1)$ is a factor of the polynomial given above?

$P(x) = (x-1) \cdot Q(x),$ $P(1) = (1-1) Q(1)$

A) -2 $P(1) = 0$

B) 0 $1 + M \cdot (1)^3 - 2 \cdot (1) + 3 = 0$

C) 1 $1 + M - 2 + 3 = 0$

D) 2 $M + 2 = 0$ $M = -2$

         $-2 \quad -2$

5

$$P(x) = mx^2 + 2nx + 7$$

$P(1) = m + 2n + 7$

If $P(-2) = P(1)$, what is the value of $m - 2n$?

$m \cdot (-2)^2 + 2n(-2) + 7 = m + 2n + 7$

A) -2 $4m - 4n + 7 = m + 2n + 7$

B) -1 $-m + 4n$ $-m + 4n$

C) 0 $\dfrac{3m}{3} = \dfrac{6n}{3}$ $m = 2n$

D) 2 $-2n \quad -2n$

             $m - 2n = 0$

6

$$Q(x) = 5(x^2 + 7x + 4) + 2(x - n)$$

$Q(0) = 5(0 + 0 + 4) + 2(0 - n)$

The polynomial $Q(x)$ is defined above. If $Q(x)$ is divisible by x, what is the value of n?

$Q(0) = 20 - 2n = 0$

A) -10 $+2n \quad +2n$

B) -2 $\dfrac{20}{2} = \dfrac{2n}{2}$

C) 0

D) 10 $n = 10$

7

$$y = ax^3 + bx + c$$

$1 = a(-1)^3 + b(-1) + c$

The polynomial given above passes through the point (-1,1). Which of the following must be true?

$1 = -a - b + c$

$-1 = a + b - c$

A) $a - b = -1$
B) $-b + c = -1 + a$
C) $a + b - c = -1$
D) $a - b - c = 1$

8

$P(x) = x^2 + 4x + 11 \qquad P(\sqrt{7} - 2) = Q$

What is the value of Q?

A) 12
B) 14
C) 22
D) 30

$P(\sqrt{7}-2) = (\sqrt{7}-2)^2 + 4(\sqrt{7}-2) + 11$

$P(\sqrt{7}-2) = 7 - 4\sqrt{7} + 4 + 4\sqrt{7} - 8 + 11$

$P(\sqrt{7}-2) = 14$

9

$$P(x,y) = 2xy^2 - 3x^2y + 4x - 5y + 2x^3y$$

$P(-1,2) = 2(-1)2^2 - 3(-1)^2 2 + 4(-1) - 5(2) + 2(-1)^3 \cdot 2$

What is the value of $P(-1,2)$?

A) -32
B) -18
C) -16
D) 12

$P(-1,2) = -8 - 6 - 4 - 10 - 4 = -32$

10

$$2(5k + 4)(3k + 2)(3k) = 0$$

$5k+4=0 \quad 3k+2=0 \quad k=0$

How many different possible values of k satisfy the equation given above?

Do NOT waste your time to solve for k.

A) One
B) Two
C) Three
D) Four

3 different values

11

If $x^2 - 2x + 3 = m$ and $-2x + 7 = n$, which of the following is the sum of the roots of $m + n$?

$m = x^2 - 2x + 3$

$+\ n = -2x + 7$

$m + n = x^2 - 4x + 10$

A) -4
B) -2
C) 4
D) 10

$x_1 = \dfrac{-b - \sqrt{\Delta}}{2a} \qquad x_2 = \dfrac{-b + \sqrt{\Delta}}{2a}$

$x_1 + x_2 = \dfrac{-b - \sqrt{\Delta}}{2a} + \dfrac{-b + \sqrt{\Delta}}{2a} = \dfrac{-b}{a}$

$x_1 + x_2 = \dfrac{-(-4)}{1} = 4$

12

$$5x^{11} + 3x^8 - A$$

When the polynomial given above is divided by $x + 1$, the remainder is 17. What is the remainder if the polynomial above is divided by $x - 1$?

A) -19
B) -11
C) 27
D) 34

$5x^{11} + 3x^8 - A = (x+1)Q(x) + R$

$5(-1)^{11} + 3(-1)^8 - A = (-1+1)Q(-1) + 17$

$-5 + 3 - A = 17$

$-2 - A = 17$
$+2 \qquad +2$

$-A = 19$

$A = -19$

$5x^{11} + 3x^8 - (-19) = (x-1)K(x) + R$

$5 \cdot (1)^{11} + 3(1)^8 + 19 = (1-1)K(1) + R$

$5 + 3 + 19 = R$

$R = 27$

CONTINUE ▶

13

$$x^2 + 6x + 15 = (x-2)(x+8) + m$$

$x^2 + 6x + 15 = x^2 + 8x - 2x - 16 + m$

Based on the polynomial equality given above, what is the value of m?

$x^2 + 6x + 15 = x^2 + 6x - 16 + m$

A) -1

$15 = -16 + m$

B) 15

$+16 \quad +16$

C) 16

$m = 31$

D) 31

14

$$(3x-5)(-2x^2 + 4x - 7)$$

If the polynomial given above is multiplied by $3x - 5$, what is the coefficient of x in the resulting polynomial?

A) -41 $3x \cdot (-7) + (-5) \cdot 4x$

B) -8 $-21x - 20x = -41x$

C) -1

D) 1

15

$$x^3 + mx + n = (x^2 + 1)Q(x) + 3x - 2$$

$x^3 = x^2 \cdot x$ Let $x^2 = -1$

According to the polynomial equation given above, what is the value of $m + n$?

$-x + mx + n = (-1+1)Q(x) + 3x - 2$

A) 2 $(m-1)x + n = 3x - 2$

B) 4

$m-1 = 3 \quad n = -2$

C) 6 $+1 \quad +1$

D) 8 $m = 4 \quad m+n = 4-2 = 2$

16

$$P(x) = 7x^4 - 3x^3 + 5x + 3$$

$$Q(x) = -4x^4 - 2x^3 - x^2 - 3x + 4$$

$2(\ldots + 3) - 3(\ldots + 4) = \ldots \; 6 - 12 = \ldots - 6$

Polynomials $P(x)$ and $Q(x)$ are given above. Find the polynomial $2P(x) - 3Q(x)$.

Constant term will be -6

A) $26x^4 + 3x^2 + 19x - 6$ $2(7x^4\ldots) - 3(-4x^4\ldots)$

B) $26x^4 + 3x^2 + 13x + 18$ $26x^4\ldots$

C) $13x^4 - 4x^3 - 2x^2 - 6x + 17$

D) $2x^4 - 12x^3 - 3x^2 + x - 6$

17

$$\frac{(x+y)^2 + (x-y)^2}{x^2 + y^2}$$

What is the simplified form of the equation above?

$\dfrac{x^2 + 2xy + y^2 + x^2 - 2xy + y^2}{x^2 + y^2}$

A) 1

B) 2

C) x $\dfrac{2(x^2 + y^2)}{(x^2 + y^2)} = 2$

D) xy

18

$$P(x) = (a-2)x^3 - (b+1)x^2 - 2x + 4$$

$$Q(x) = 5x^3 + 2x^2 - cx + d - 3$$

The polynomials $P(x)$ and $Q(x)$ are given above. If the polynomials are equal, then what is the value of $a + b + c + d$?

$a - 2 = 5 \quad -b-1 = 2 \quad -c = -2$

$+2 \quad +2 \quad\quad +1 \quad +1 \quad\quad c = 2$

A) 7 $a = 7$ $-b = 3$

B) 8 $b = -3$ $d - 3 = 4$

                       $+3 \quad +3$

C) 11 $d = 7$

D) 13 $a + b + c + d = 7 - 3 + 2 + 7 = 13$

19

If $h(x-2) = 5x^2 + 3x - 9$, then which of the following defines $h(x)$?

$x \rightarrow x+2$

$h(x+2-2) = 5(x+2)^2 + 3(x+2) - 9$

A) $5x^2 + 3x - 7$ $h(x) = 5(x^2+4x+4) + 3x - 3$

B) $5x^2 + 3x - 11$

C) $5x^2 + 23x + 17$ $h(x) = 5x^2 + 20x + 17$

D) $5x^2 + 23x + 23$

20

$$P(x) = ax^4 + bx^2 + c$$

$P(1) = a(1)^4 + b(1)^2 + c$

The polynomial $P(x)$ is defined above. If $P(1)$ is equal to -12, what is the value of $P(-1)$?

$a + b + c = -12$

A) -12 $P(-1) = a(-1)^4 + b(-1)^2 + c$

B) 12 $P(-1) = a + b + c = -12$

C) 0

D) It can not be determined.

21

$$(x-2)P(x) = 3x^2 - mx + 3m + 2$$

$(2-2)P(2) = 3 \cdot 2^2 - 2m + 3m + 2$

Given the polynomial above, what is the value of $P(1)$?

$0 = 12 + m + 2$

$0 = 14 + m$

$\frac{-14 \quad -14}{}$ $m = -14$

A) -20

B) -16 $(1-2)P(1) = 3 \cdot 1^2 - (-14)1 + 3(-14) + 2$

C) 23 $-P(1) = 3 + 14 - 42 + 2$

D) 33 $-P(1) = -23$ $P(1) = 23$

22

$$P(x) = 2x^2 \quad Q(x) = 4x^3$$

$$P(3x^5) \cdot Q(2x^4) = m \cdot x^n$$

$2(3x^5)^2 \cdot 4(2x^4)^3 = m \cdot x^n$

Given the operations with polynomials above, what is the value of $m + n$?

$2 \cdot (9x^{10}) \cdot 4(8x^{12}) = m \cdot x^n$

A) 70

B) 576 $576 x^{22} = m \cdot x^n$

C) 590 $m = 576 \quad n = 22$

D) 598 $m+n = 576 + 22 = 598$

23

$$3x^2 - 4y^2 = 11$$

$$+ \quad 4 \cdot x^2 + 4y^2 = 13 \cdot 4$$
$$\overline{7y^2 = 63}$$

If $x > 0$ and $y > 0$ in the equations given above, what is the value of $x^y + y^x$?

$\frac{7}{7}y^2 = \frac{63}{7} \quad y^2 = 9 \quad y = 3$

A) 6 $x^2 + 3^2 = 13 \quad x^2 + 9 = 13$

B) 12 $\quad -9 \quad -9$

C) 17 $x^2 = 4 \quad x = 2$

D) 18 $x^y + y^x = 2^3 + 3^2 = 8 + 9 = 17$

24

$$(x-a)^2 = x^2 - 6x + b$$

Based on the equation given above, what is the value of $a + b$?

$x^2 - 2ax + a^2 = x^2 - 6x + b$

A) 3

B) 6 $\frac{-2a}{-2} = \frac{-6}{-2} \quad a = 3$

C) 9 $b = a^2 \quad b = 3^2 = 9$

D) 12 $a + b = 3 + 9 = 12$

25

If $x^2 + mx + n = (x - 2)(x + 6)$, what is the value of mn?

$x^2 + mx + n = x^2 + 6x - 2x - 12$

A) -48 $x^2 + mx + n = x^2 + 4x - 12$

B) -12 $m = 4$ $n = -12$

C) 4

D) 24 $m \cdot n = 4 \cdot -12 = -48$

26

$$P(x) = ax^2 + bx + c$$

The polynomial $P(x)$ is defined above. If $P(1)$ is equal to $P(-1)$, what is the value of b?

$a(1)^2 + b(1) + c = a(-1)^2 + b(-1) + c$

A) -1

B) 1 $a + b + c = a - b + c$
          $-a + b - c$ $-a + b - c$

C) 0 $2b = 0$ $b = 0$

D) It can not be determined.

27

$$P(ax) = x^4 - 2x^3 + x + b$$

$ax = -2a$ $x = -2$

If $P(-2a) = 44$, then what is the value of b?

$P(-2a) = (-2)^4 - 2(-2)^3 - 2 + b = 44$

A) 10

B) 14 $16 - 2(-8) - 2 + b = 44$

C) 42 $16 + 16 - 2 + b = 44$

D) 46 $30 + b = 44$
               -30 -30

               $b = 14$

28

$$P(x + 2y, x - 3y) = y^2 + 2x - m$$

What is the value of m if $P(7,-3)$ is equal to 8?

$3 \cdot (x + 2y = 7)$ $3x + 6y = 21$

A) 0 $2(x - 3y = -3)$ $\underline{+ 2x - 6y = -6}$

B) 1 $\frac{5}{5}x = \frac{15}{5}$ $x = 3$

C) 2 $x + 2y = 7$ $\frac{3 + 2y = 7}{-3}$ $\frac{2y}{2} = \frac{4}{2}$ $y = 2$

D) 5 $P(7,-3) = 2^2 + 2 \cdot 3 - m = 8$
         $4 + 6 - m = 8$
         $10 - m = 8$ $-m = -2$
         -10 -10 $m = 2$

29

$$P(x) = (3x^3 - 4x^2 + x - 5) \cdot (2x^2 - 5x + 1)$$

$$P(x) = ax^5 + bx^4 + cx^3 + dx^2 + ex + f$$

Given the polynomial $P(x)$ above, what is the value of $b + c$?

$bx^4 = 3x^3 \cdot (-5x) - 4x^2 \cdot 2x^2$

A) 2 $bx^4 = -23x^4$ $b = -23$

B) 23 $cx^3 = -4x^2(-5x) + x \cdot (2x^2) + 3x^3 \cdot 1$

C) 25 $cx^3 = 25x^3$ $c = 25$

D) 48 $b + c = -23 + 25 = 2$

30

$$x^2 + 4x + c = 0$$
$$ax^2 + bx + c$$

If the equation above has two distinct real solutions, which of the following can not be the value of c?

$\Delta > 0$ $b^2 - 4ac > 0$ $4^2 - 4 \cdot 1 \cdot c > 0$

A) -1 $16 - 4c > 0$
          -16 -16

B) 1

C) 3 $\frac{-4c}{-4} > \frac{-16}{-4}$

D) 5 $c < 4$

31

$$P(x)=x^3-(m+1)x^2+(n+1)x+k-5$$

$$Q(x)=(x^2-3)(x+1)$$

$Q(x) = x^3 + 1x^2 - 3x - 3$

If the polynomilas $P(x)$ and $Q(x)$ are equal, then what is the value of $\frac{m-n}{k}$?

$k-5=-3$, $k=2$; $-m-1=1$, $-m=2$, $m=-2$; $n+1=-3$, $n=-4$

A) 1
B) 2
C) 3
D) 4

$\frac{m-n}{k} = \frac{-2-(-4)}{2} = \frac{2}{2} = 1$

32

$$x^2+ax-5=(x+1)(bx+c)$$

In the equation above is *x* a real number. What is the value of *a* +*b* +*c*?

$x^2+ax-5 = bx^2+cx+bx+c$

$1x^2+ax-5 = bx^2+(b+c)x+c$

A) -8
B) -5
C) 1
D) 9

$b=1$, $a=b+c$, $a=1-5$, $a=-4$, $c=-5$

$a+b+c=-4+1-5=-8$

33

$$P(x)=x^3+4x^2+2mx-5$$

$P(1)=1^3+4\cdot(1)^2+2m\cdot 1-5=4$

When the polynomial given above is divided by (*x*-1) the remainder is 4. What will be the remainder when the polynomial is divided by (*x*-2)?

$1+4+2m-5=4$, $\frac{2}{2}m=\frac{4}{2}$, $m=2$

A) 11
B) 27
C) 32
D) 37

$P(2)=2^3+4(2)^2+2\cdot 2\cdot 2-5$

$P(2)=8+16+8-5$

$P(2)=27$

34

$(4x^2-\frac{3}{2}x+5)$ is multiplied by $(8x+\frac{1}{4})$. What is the coefficient of x^2?

A) −11
B) 1
C) 12
D) 32

$4x^2\cdot\frac{1}{4} - \frac{3}{2}x\cdot 8x$

$x^2-12x^2=-11x^2$

35

$$P(x+2y,x-3y)=y^2+3x-5$$

According to the polynomial equation given above, what is the value of P(7,2)?

$x+2y=7$, $+\ -x+3y=-2$, $\frac{5}{5}y=\frac{5}{5}$, $y=1$

$x+2\cdot 1=7$, $x=5$

A) 6
B) 7
C) 9
D) 11

$P(7,2)=1^2+3\cdot 5-5=11$

36

$$(a^2b-2b^2+5ab^2)-(-a^2b+8ab^2+3b^2)$$

$a^2b-2b^2+5ab^2+a^2b-8ab^2-3b^2$

Which of the following is equivalent to the expression above? $2a^2b-3ab^2-5b^2$

A) b^2+13ab^2
B) $2a^2b+b^2-3a^2b$
C) $-3a^2b-5b^2$
D) $2a^2b-3ab^2-5b^2$

37

$$P(x) = 3x^3 + 4x$$
$$Q(x) = -2x^4 + x^3 + x^2$$

$$P(x^2) = 3(x^2)^3 + 4x^2 = 3x^6 + 4x^2$$

Polynomials $P(x)$ and $Q(x)$ are given above.

Find the polynomial $P(x^2) + Q(x)$.

$$3x^6 + 4x^2 - 2x^4 + x^3 + x^2$$

A) $3x^6 + 4x^5 - 2x^4$

B) $3x^5 + 4x^4 + 2x^3$

C) $3x^6 - 2x^4 + x^3 + 5x^2$

D) $-2x^4 + 4x^3 + x^2 + 4x$

38

$$a^2 + 16 - 2a = 6a$$
$$-6a \quad -6a$$

What is the value of $2a - 1$ based on the equation above?

$$a^2 - 8a + 16 = 0$$

A) 7 $\qquad (a-4)^2 = 0$

B) 9 $\qquad \begin{array}{l} a - 4 = 0 \\ +4 \quad +4 \end{array} \quad a = 4$

C) 11

D) 17 $\qquad 2a - 1 = 2 \cdot 4 - 1 = 7$

39

$$x^2 + ax - 5 = (x+1)(bx+c)$$

$$x^2 + ax - 5 = bx^2 + cx + bx + c$$

According to the polynomial equation given above, what is the value of $a + b + c$?

$$1x^2 + ax - 5 = bx^2 + (b+c)x + c$$

A) -9 $\quad b = 1 \qquad a = b + c \qquad c = -5$

B) -8 $\qquad\qquad a = 1 - 5$

C) 0 $\qquad\qquad a = -4$

D) 8 $\qquad a + b + c = -4 + 1 - 5 = -8$

40

$$P(x) = x^2 + \tfrac{1}{2}x - 4 \qquad Q(x) = -2x^2 - 5x + 1$$
$$P(-2) = (-2)^2 - 2 - 4 \quad Q(-2) = -2(-2)^2 - 5(-2) + 1$$
$$n \cdot P(-2) = Q(-2)$$
$$P(-2) = -2 \qquad\qquad Q(-2) = 3$$

Based on the polynomial equations given above, what is the value of n?

A) -0.5 $\qquad \dfrac{n \cdot (-2)}{-2} = \dfrac{3}{-2}$

B) 1

C) -1.5 $\qquad n = -1.5$

D) 2

41

When polynomial P(x) is divided by (x + 2), the remainder is 3. Which of the following must be true about P(x)?

A) $P(2) = 3 \qquad P(x) = (x+2)Q(x) + R$

B) $P(3) = 2 \qquad P(-2) = (-2+2)Q(-2) + 3$

C) $P(-2) = 3 \qquad P(-2) = 3$

D) $P(-3) = -2$

42

If $a = 3x^2 - x + 2$, $b = x^2 + 5$, $c = 4x - 7$, then find $2a - (3b + c)$?

$$2(3x^2 - x + 2) - (3(x^2 + 5) + 4x - 7)$$

A) $2x^2 - 5x - 10 \quad 6x^2 - 2x + 4 - (3x^2 + 15 + 4x - 7)$

B) $3x^2 + 2x - 18$

C) $3x^2 - 6x - 4 \quad 6x^2 - 2x + 4 - 3x^2 - 15 - 4x + 7$

D) $9x^2 + 2x + 12 \quad 3x^2 - 6x - 4$

43

$$P(x) = ax + b$$

$$P(2x + 1) + P(3x - 1) = 5x + 6$$

$a(2x+1)+b + a(3x-1)+b = 5x+6$

What is the value of $P(0)$?

$5ax + 2b = 5x + 6$

$\frac{5a}{5} = \frac{5}{5}$ $\quad \frac{2b}{2} = \frac{6}{2}$

$a = 1$ $\quad b = 3$

$P(0) = 1 \cdot 0 + 3 = 3$

A) -2
B) -1
C) 3
D) 6

44

$$144x^2 - 36 = a^2(bx - c)(bx + c)$$

$144x^2 - 36 = a^2(b^2x^2 - c^2)$

If a, b, and c are positive integers, which of the following can be the value of $a + b + c$?

$144x^2 - 36 = a^2b^2x^2 - a^2c^2$

$ab = 12$	$ac = 6$	$a+b+c$
1 12	1 6	$1+12+6=19$ ✓
3 4	3 2	$3+4+2=9$ ✓
2 6	2 3	$2+6+3=11$ ✓

A) 9
B) 11
C) 19
D) All of the above

45

$$2x - 4 = ax(x-1) + bx(x+1) + c(x^2 - 1)$$

$0x^2 + 2x - 4 = (a+b+c)x^2 + (-a+b)x - c$

What is the value of $a \cdot b \cdot c$?

$a+b+c=0$ $\quad -a+b=2$ $\quad -c=-4$

$a+b+4=0$ $\quad a+b=-4$ $\quad c=4$

$a+b=-4$ $\quad \frac{2b}{2}=\frac{-2}{2}$ $\quad b=-1$

$a-1=-4$ $\quad a=-3$ $\quad a \cdot b \cdot c = -3 \cdot -1 \cdot 4$

$a \cdot b \cdot c = 12$

A) 6
B) 8
C) 10
D) 12

46

If $x^2 = 4$ and $y^2 = 9$, which of the following is a possible value of $(x + 4y)^2$?

$x = +2$ or -2 $\quad y = +3$ or -3

$(x+4y)^2 = x^2 + 2 \cdot x \cdot 4y + 16y^2$

$= 4 + 8xy + 16 \cdot 9$

$= 148 + 8xy$

$= 148 + 8 \cdot 6$ or $148 - 8 \cdot 6$

196 or 100

A) 40
B) 100
C) 144
D) 148

47

$$a^2 - b^2 - a + b$$

$(a+b)(a-b) - (a-b)$

If one of the factors of the expression above is $a - b$, then what is the other factor of it?

$(a-b)(a+b-1)$

A) $a+b-1$
B) $a+b+1$
C) $a-b+1$
D) $-a+2b+1$

48

$$\frac{a^8 + 4a^2 - 8}{a^2 + 2}$$

What is the result of the operation given above?

$a^6 - 2a^4 \ldots$

$a^2 + 2 \,)\, a^8 + 4a^2 - 8$

$-a^8 \mp 2a^6$

$-2a^6 + 4a^2 - 8$

$+2a^6 + 4a^4$

A) $a^6 + 4a^2 - 4$
B) $a^6 - a^5 - 4$
C) $a^6 - 2a^4 + 4a^2 - 4$
D) $a^6 - a^5 + 4a^4 - 4$

CONTINUE ▶

49

If $p(x)=ax^2+bx+c$ and $p(1)=8$, $p(-1)=6$ then find $a+c$.

$P(1)=a+b+c=8$

$P(-1)=a(-1)^2+b(-1)+c=6$

$a+b+c=8$

$+\ a-b+c=6$

$\frac{2(a+c)}{2}=\frac{14}{2}$ $a+c=7$

A) 2
B) 7
C) 14
D) 48

50

$P(x)=x^2-2x+5 \quad Q(x)=x^3-5x+2$

$R(x)=3P(4x^3)+4Q(5x^4)$

The polynomial $R(x)$ is defined in terms of polynomials $P(x)$ and $Q(x)$. What is the constant term of $R(x)$?

Focus on the constant term

$R(x)=3\cdot(\ldots\ldots+5)+4(\ldots\ldots+2)$

$R(x)=\ldots\ldots+15+8$

$R(x)=\ldots\ldots+23$

A) 7
B) 23
C) 30
D) 100

51

$h(x) = ax^2 + bx + c$

$h(0)=a\cdot0^2+b\cdot0+c=7$ $c=7$

If $h(0) = 7$, $h(1) = 19$, and $h(-1) = 13$, then what is the value of $a + b + c$?

$h(1)=a\cdot1^2+b\cdot1+7=19$, -7 -7; $a+b=12$

$h(-1)=a(-1)^2+b(-1)+7=13$, -7 -7; $a-b=6$

$a+b=12$

$+\ a-b=6$

$\frac{2a}{2}=\frac{18}{2}$ $a=9$

$9+b=12$, -9 -9; $b=3$

$a+b+c=9+3+7=19$

A) 3
B) 7
C) 9
D) 19

52

$(-x^2+3x+7)(6x^5-3x^4+x^2+2x-5)$

After the multiplication of the polynomials given above, what will be the coefficent of the term x^3?

You don't need to multiply everything. Just multiply the terms that gives x^3.

$-x^2\cdot2x$ $+3x\cdot x^2$

$-2x^3+3x^3=1x^3$

A) -2
B) 1
C) 3
D) 5

53

$p(x)=2(3x^2+12x+15)-6(x-m)$

$p(x)=\ldots\ldots+30+6m$ constant term

The polynomial $p(x)$ is defined above. If m is a constant and $p(x)$ is divisible by x, then what is the value of m?

If $p(x)$ is divisible by x then, constant term must be zero.

$30+6m=0$, -30 -30

$\frac{6m}{6}=\frac{-30}{6}$ $m=-5$

A) -3
B) -2.5
C) -5
D) 5

54

$a+b=4$

$b-c=3$

What is the value of $ab-ac+b^2-bc$?

$ab-ac+b^2-bc$

$a(b-c)+b(b-c)$

$(b-c)\cdot(a+b)$

$3\cdot4=12$

A) 4
B) 8
C) 12
D) 16

55

$$P(x)=x^4+\frac{1}{2}x^3+x^2+ax$$

$P(x)=(x^2+1)Q(x)+R \quad R=0$

If the polynomial given above is divisible by x^2+1, then what is the value of a?

$x^2=-1$

A) $-\frac{1}{3}$

B) $-\frac{1}{2}$

C) $\frac{1}{2}$

D) $\frac{1}{3}$

$(x^2)^2+\frac{1}{2}x^2\cdot x+x^2+ax$

$(-1)^2+\frac{1}{2}(-1)\cdot x+(-1)+ax=0$

$ax-\frac{x}{2}=0$

$+\frac{x}{2} \quad +\frac{x}{2}$

$ax=\frac{x}{2} \quad a=\frac{1}{2}$

56

$$\frac{x^2+ax+b}{x^2+11x+28}\cdot\frac{x^2+4x-21}{x^2-9}=\frac{x+2}{x+3}$$

What is the value of $a+b$?

$\frac{x^2+ax+b}{(x+7)(x+4)}\cdot\frac{(x+7)(x-3)}{(x+3)(x-3)}=\frac{x+2}{x+3}$

A) 10

B) 12

C) 14

D) 16

$x^2+ax+b=(x+4)\cdot(x+2)$

$x^2+ax+b=x^2+6x+8$

$a=6$

$+\ b=8$

$a+b=14$

57

$$x(x-4)(x+6)(x-2)$$

$\ldots\ldots +48x$

Which of the following is the equivalent to the polynomial above? Don't multiply the terms. Focus on the last term.

A) x^4+12x^3

B) $x^3-4x^2+4x-48$

C) $x^4-4x^3+4x^2-48x$

D) x^4-28x^2+48x

58

$$x^2-4y=-7$$
$$+\ y^2-2x=2$$

$x^2+y^2-4y-2x=-5$

What is the value of $x+y$?

$x^2-2x+1 \quad +y^2-4y+4=-5+1+4$

$(x-1)^2+(y-2)^2=0$

$x=1 \quad y=2$

$x+y=1+2=3$

A) 3

B) 4

C) 5

D) 7

59

$$A=a+b+c$$
$$+\ B=a-b-c$$

$(A+B)=2a$

Given the equations above find the value of A^2-B^2.

$(A-B)=a+b+c-a+b+c=2(b+c)$

$A^2-B^2=(A+B)(A-B)$

$A^2-B^2=2a\cdot 2(b+c)$

$=4a(b+c)$

A) $4a(b+c)$

B) $4b(a+c)$

C) $2c(a+b)$

D) $2a(b-c)$

60

$$P(x)=x^3+24$$

What is the remainder when the polynomial given above is divided by $x-2$?

$x^3+24=(x-2)Q(x)+R$

$2^3+24=(2-2)Q(2)+R$

$32=R$

CONTINUE ▶

61

What real value of x makes the equation $x^3 - 5x^2 + 2x - 10 = 0$ true?

$x^2(x-5)+2(x-5)=(x^2+2)(x-5)=0$

$x=5$

62

Alexis has finished weaving a blanket. She made the blanket length four feet greater than twice its width.

$w(2w+4)=70$ w $l=2w+4$

If the area covered by the blanket is 70 square feet, how many feet is the length longer than the width of the blanket?

$2w^2+4w-70=0$ $l=2w+4$

$w^2+2w-35=0$ $l=2\cdot5+4$

$(w+7)(w-5)=0$ $l=14$

$w=5$ $l-w=14-5=9$

63

$$P(x)=5x^2-(a+3)x+14$$

$$Q(x)=(b+2)x^2-2x+c+9$$

If polynomial $P(x)$ is equal to the polynomial $Q(x)$, then what is the value of $a+b+c$?

$b+2=5$, -2 -2, $b=3$

$-(a+3)=-2$, $a+3=2$, -3 -3, $a=-1$

$c+9=14$, -9 -9, $c=5$

$a+b+c=-1+3+5=7$

64

$$\frac{2x+1}{x^2-5x+6}=\frac{A}{x-3}+\frac{B}{x-2}$$

$(x-2)$ $(x-3)$

Based on the expression given above what is the value of A - B?

$2x+1=A(x-2)+B(x-3)$

$2\cdot2+1=A(2-2)+B(2-3)$

$5=-B$ $B=-5$

$2\cdot3+1=A(3-2)+B(3-3)$

$7=A$ $A-B=7-(-5)=12$

65

$$3x^4+8x^3+12x^2+5x-m$$

For what value of m, the polynomial above is divisible by $x+2$? Remainder must be zero.

$3x^4+8x^3+12x^2+5x-m=(x+2)Q(x)+R$

$3(-2)^4+8(-2)^3+12(-2)^2+5(-2)-m=(-2+2)Q(-2)+0$

$3\cdot16+8\cdot(-8)+12\cdot4-10-m=0$

$48-64+48-10-m=0$

$22-m=0$ $m=22$

66

If $a+b=4$ and c-$d=6$, then what is the value of $3(bc\text{-}ad\text{-}bd\text{+}ac)$?

$3(bc+ac-ad-bd)=3(c(a+b)-d(a+b))$

$3(a+b)(c-d)$

$3\cdot4\cdot6=72$

CONTINUE ▶

67

$$Q(x) = ax^2 + bx + c$$
$$Q(x-1) = (x-4)^2$$

Based on the polynomials given above find the value of $a+b+c$?

$a(x-1)^2 + b(x-1) + c = (x-4)^2$

$a(x^2-2x+1) + bx - b + c = x^2 - 8x + 16$

$ax^2 + (b-2a)x + a - b + c = 1 \cdot x^2 - 8x + 16$

$a = 1$ $\quad$ $b - 2a = -8$ $\quad$ $a - b + c = 16$

$b - 2 = -8$ $\quad$ $1 - (-6) + c = 16$

$+2 \quad +2$ $\quad$ $7 + c = 16$

$b = -6$ $\quad$ $-7 \quad -7$

$c = 9$

$a + b + c = 1 - 6 + 9 = 4$

68

$$P(x) = 3x^2 - 5x - 7 + c$$

If $P(1.5) = 19$ in the polynomial given above, then what is the value of $P(-0.5)$?

$3 \cdot (1.5)^2 - 5 \cdot (1.5) - 7 + c = 19$

$3 \cdot (2.25) - 7.5 - 7 + c = 19$

$6.75 - 14.5 + c = 19$

$-7.75 + c = 19$ $\quad$ $c = 26.75$

$+7.75 \quad +7.75$

$P(-0.5) = 3 \cdot (-0.5)^2 - 5 \cdot (-0.5) - 7 + 26.75$

$P(-0.5) = 0.75 + 2.5 - 7 + 26.75 = 23$

Math Test – Calculator

DIRECTIONS

For multiple choice questions, choose the best answers from the choices after you solve the questions. Check your answers from the answer key.

For free responce questions, find your answer, write it in the space provided below and finally check it from the answer key.

NOTES

1. Calculator **is allowed**.
2. All variables are real numbers unless otherwise indicated.
3. Figures of this test are drawn to scale unless otherwise indicated.
4. Figures of this test lie in a plane.
5. Unless otherwise stated, the domain of function *f* is the set of all real numbers *x* for which *f*(*x*) is a real number

REFERENCE

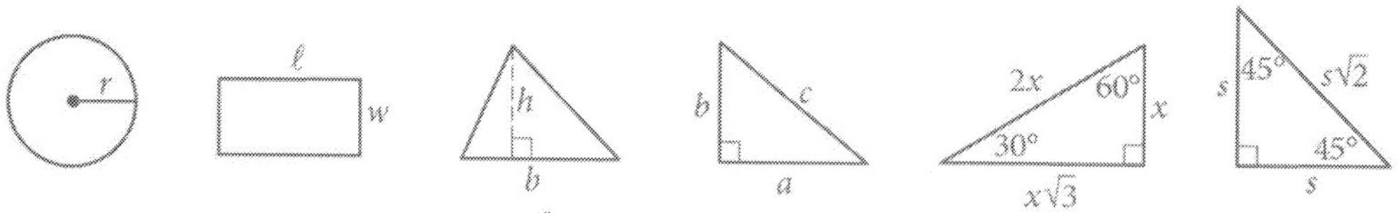

$A = \pi r^2$ $C = 2\pi r$ | $A = \ell w$ | $A = \frac{1}{2}bh$ | $c^2 = a^2 + b^2$ | Special Right Triangles

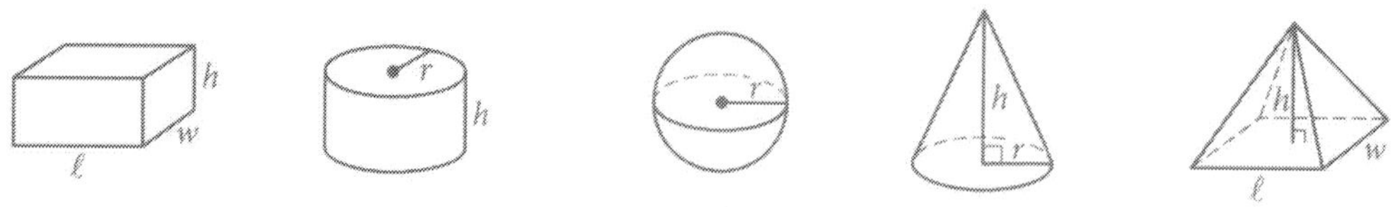

$V = \ell wh$ | $V = \pi r^2 h$ | $V = \frac{4}{3}\pi r^3$ | $V = \frac{1}{3}\pi r^2 h$ | $V = \frac{1}{3}\ell wh$

The number of degrees of a circle is 360.

The number of radians of a circle is 2π.

The sum of the angles of a triangle is 180 degrees.

CONTINUE ▶

1

$$\frac{1+10+100+1000}{0.001+0.01+0.1+1}$$

What is the value of the operation given above?

A) 10
B) 100
C) 1,000
D) 10,000

2

$$3(x - 2) + 2(x - 2) = -20$$

What is the value of $(x - 2)$?

A) -6
B) -4
C) -3.6
D) -2

3

$$\left(2-\frac{y}{y-1}\right)\div\frac{y-2}{5}$$

What is the simplified form of the equation above?

A) $\frac{5}{y-1}$
B) $\frac{y-2}{y-1}$
C) $\frac{2y-1}{y-1}$
D) $\frac{1}{y-1}$

4

$$\frac{2x}{x+3}\div\frac{12}{3x+9}$$

Which of the following is equivalent to the expression above given that $x \neq -3$?

A) $\frac{x}{2}$
B) $2x$
C) $3x$
D) $8x$

5

$$3x - 2 = 8$$

What is the value of $12x + 8$?

A) 24
B) 32
C) 40
D) 48

6

$$\frac{3}{x-2}+\frac{5}{2x-4}=\frac{11}{12}$$

Based on the expression above, what is the value of $2x - 4$?

A) 6
B) 8
C) 12
D) 16

CONTINUE ▶

7

$$\frac{0.004+0.04+0.4+4}{2+20+200+2000}$$

What is the value of the operation above?

A) 2
B) 10^{-3}
C) 2.10^{-3}
D) 2000

8

$$\frac{1}{\frac{1}{x+1}+\frac{1}{x+2}}$$

Which of the following is equivalent to the expression above?

A) $\frac{x^2+3x+2}{2x+3}$

B) $2x+3$

C) x^2+3x+2

D) $\frac{2x+3}{x^2+3x+2}$

9

The denominator of a fraction is 4 times its numerator. If 6 is added to both the numerator and denominator, then the value of the fraction is 0.5.

What is the initial sum of the numerator and denominator of the fraction?

A) 5
B) 10
C) 15
D) 20

10

$$\frac{\frac{m}{n}}{5} \div \frac{m}{\frac{n}{5}}$$

If m and n are non zero integers, what is the value of the operation given above?

A) 0.04
B) 1
C) 5
D) 25

11

$$\frac{4}{0.01}+\frac{0.4}{0.04}$$

What is the equivalent of the expression above?

A) 110
B) 114
C) 401
D) 410

12

If $x^2 - kx + 4$ is a perfect square, then what is the value of k^2?

A) -2
B) 2
C) 4
D) 16

13

If $ab = \frac{1}{3}$, then what is the value of $\left(a-\frac{1}{b}\right)\left(\frac{1}{a}-b\right)$?

A) $-\frac{1}{3}$
B) -1
C) $-\frac{4}{3}$
D) $\frac{5}{3}$

14

$$\frac{a+b-1}{ab} = K$$

$$a = \frac{x}{x+y} \qquad b = \frac{y}{x+y}$$

What is the value of K?

A) -2
B) -1
C) 0
D) It can not be determined.

15

If $a = -2$ and $b = 2^{-1}$, then what is the value of $\frac{ab}{a^2 + 2b}$?

A) $-\frac{1}{2}$

B) $-\frac{1}{5}$

C) $\frac{1}{5}$

D) 1

16

$$\frac{5(k+2)-4}{6} = \frac{8-(3-k)}{3}$$

What is the value of k in the equation above?

A) $\frac{12}{21}$

B) $\frac{4}{3}$

C) $\frac{3}{2}$

D) $\frac{16}{3}$

17

$$127^2 - 101^2 = 26k$$

What is the value of k in the equation given above?

A) 176

B) 187

C) 217

D) 228

18

$$\frac{1-\frac{1}{x}}{1+\frac{1}{x}} = 3$$

What is the value of x?

A) -3

B) -2

C) -1

D) 1

19

$$a-b=b-c=4 \qquad a^2+c^2-2b^2=K$$

What is the value of K in the equation given above?

A) 16
B) 25
C) 28
D) 32

20

$$\frac{x^2+5x-7}{x^3+3x^2-4x}$$

What values of x make the expression above undefined?

A) 0,1,4
B) -4,1
C) -4,1,0
D) 4,0,-1

21

$$\frac{156^2+244^2+312\cdot 244}{2^3\cdot 5^3}$$

What is the value of the operation given above?

A) 16
B) 40
C) 160
D) 400

22

$$\frac{x^2-7x+12}{8x+88x^2+240x}$$

Which of the following value of x makes the fraction above undefined?

A) $-\frac{30}{11}$
B) –4
C) 3
D) $-\frac{31}{11}$

23

$$(1003-105)(1003+105)+105^2=A$$

What is the value of A?

A) 1003
B) 1108
C) 105^2
D) 1003^2

24

$$\frac{m}{n-1}+\left(\frac{m}{n-1}\right)^2+\left(\frac{m}{n-1}\right)^3$$

If $m + 2n = 2$, then what is the value of the operation given above?

A) -6
B) -2
C) 8
D) 14

CONTINUE ▶

25

$$\frac{a}{b}+\frac{b}{a}=4 \qquad \frac{a^2}{b^2}+\frac{b^2}{a^2}=K$$

What is the value of K?

A) 8
B) 12
C) 14
D) 16

26

The expression $\frac{3x-4}{x+2}$ is equivalent to which of the following ?

A) $3-\frac{10}{x+2}$
B) $3+\frac{2}{x+2}$
C) $3+\frac{10}{x+2}$
D) $3-\frac{2}{x+2}$

27

$$\frac{4y^2-100}{y+5}=12$$

What is the value of y ?

A) -2
B) 8
C) 12
D) 17

28

$$x^2+y^2=49-2xy$$

According to the equation given above, what is the positive value of $x+y$?

A) 4
B) 5
C) 6
D) 7

29

$$a^2+ab=5$$
$$b^2+ab=20$$

What is the positive value of $a+b$?

A) 2
B) 3
C) 4
D) 5

30

$$\frac{6x+20}{x+2}=A+\frac{B}{x+2}$$

Based on the expression above, find $A+B$.

A) 14
B) 20
C) 26
D) 28

31

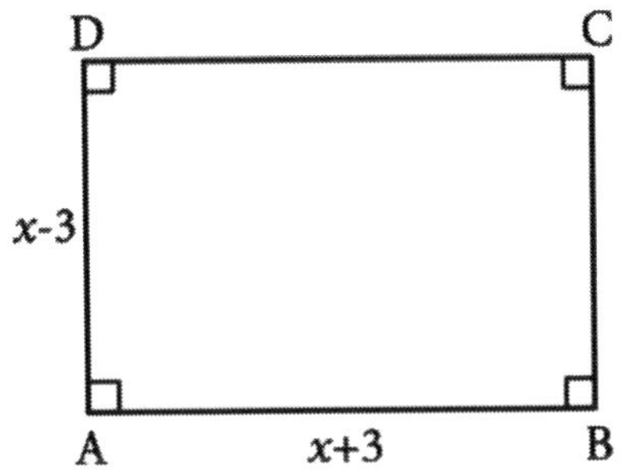

If the area of rectangle ABCD is 36, then what is the perimeter of ABCD?

A) 12
B) $6\sqrt{5}$
C) $12\sqrt{5}$
D) $12\sqrt{5}-6$

32

$$(444)^2-(333)^2=111^2\cdot k$$

What is the value of k?

A) 1
B) 2
C) 7
D) 49

33

$$\frac{m-1}{m-3}=\frac{m-5}{m-4}$$

According to the equation above what is the value of m?

A) $\frac{8}{5}$
B) $\frac{13}{4}$
C) $\frac{9}{4}$
D) $\frac{11}{3}$

34

If $a - b = 7$ and $ab = 3$, then what is the value of $2a^2b^3 - 2a^3b^2$?

A) -252
B) -126
C) -84
D) 294

CONTINUE ▶

35

$$\frac{x(y+z)+z(y-x)}{x^2+xy+xz+yz}$$

What is the simplified form of the equation above?

A) $\frac{x}{x+y}$

B) $\frac{y}{x+y}$

C) $\frac{z}{x+z}$

D) $\frac{y}{y+z}$

36

$$\frac{1+\frac{1}{x}}{\frac{1}{x^2}-1}$$

What is the simplified form of the equation above?

A) $\frac{1}{x-1}$

B) $\frac{1}{1-x}$

C) $\frac{-x}{x-1}$

D) $\frac{x-1}{x}$

37

$$(x+4+y)^2+(x-8-y)^2=0$$

Given the equation above, what is the value of xy?

A) -6

B) 4

C) 2

D) -12

38

$$\frac{240^2-60^2}{80^2-20^2}$$

What is the simplified form of the equation given above?

A) 3

B) 6

C) 9

D) 12

39

$$(18 - a)(18 + a) + 36 = 324$$

What is the value of *a*?

A) 6
B) 36
C) 288
D) 360

40

$$a+3=b+4$$

$$\frac{1}{a+3}+\frac{1}{b+4}=1$$

Based on the equations above, what is the value of *a* + *b*?

A) -1
B) -2
C) -3
D) -4

41

$$x^2 - y^2 = 29$$

If *x* and *y* are positive integers, then what is the value of 2*x* - *y*?

A) 14
B) 15
C) 16
D) 30

42

If $x^2 + y^2 + 2x - 6y + 10 = 0$, then what is the value of *x* + *y*?

A) -1
B) -2
C) 2
D) 4

43

$$(x+2)^2 + y^2 + 9 = 6y$$

What is the sum of the values of *x* and *y* that satisfy the equation given above?

A) -1
B) 1
C) 5
D) 6

44

$$\frac{5}{2x+1}+\frac{2x+1}{5}=\frac{17}{5}+\frac{5}{17}$$

What is the value of *x* that satisfies the equation given above?

A) 5
B) 7
C) 8
D) 9

45

$$\frac{x}{y}=\frac{y}{z} \qquad x^2+xz+2xy=4$$

Based on the equations given above, what is the value of $x + y$?

A) 1
B) 2
C) 4
D) 16

46

$$x^2+y^2-6x+8y+69$$

What is the minimum value of the expression given above if both x and y are integers?

A) 36
B) 39
C) 42
D) 44

47

$$\left[\left(\frac{1}{x}+\frac{1}{y}\right)^2-\left(\frac{1}{x}-\frac{1}{y}\right)^2\right]\cdot xy$$

What is the result of the operation given above?

A) -1
B) 0
C) 1
D) 4

48

$$xy=2 \qquad x+y=4$$
$$\frac{x}{y}+\frac{y}{x}=M$$

What is the value of M?

A) 6
B) 8
C) 10
D) 12

49

$$2x-y=4 \qquad 3a+b=5$$

According to the equations given above, what is the value of $6ax + 2bx - 3ay - yb$?

A) 1
B) 9
C) 20
D) 40

50

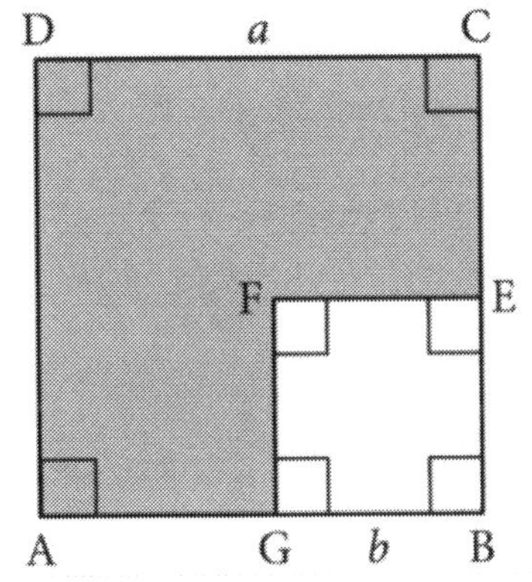

ABCD and GBEF are squares. If the shaded area is $40cm^2$ and AG = 4cm, then what is the value of a?

A) 4

B) 6

C) 7

D) 10

51

$$\frac{a-b}{a+b}=\frac{3}{7}$$

Based on the equation above, find the value of $\frac{a^2+b^2}{a^2-b^2}$.

A) $\frac{29}{21}$

B) $\frac{28}{27}$

C) $\frac{15}{17}$

D) $\frac{21}{25}$

52

$$\frac{5x}{x-3}+\frac{2x}{2x-6}=\frac{54}{3x-9}$$

What value of x satisfies the equation given above?

A) 3

B) 6

C) There is no solution.

D) There are infinitely many solutions.

53

If $a^2 - a = b^2 - b$, and $ab = -1$, then what is the value of $a^2 + b^2$?

A) 3

B) 4

C) 5

D) 6

CONTINUE ▶

54

$$\frac{a^2-(b-1)^2}{a+b-1}=17$$

What is the value of *a* - *b*?

A) 13

B) 15

C) 16

D) 18

55

$$(a-b)^2+4ab$$

Find the value of the expression above for $a=\frac{11}{24}$ and $b=\frac{13}{24}$.

A) 1

B) $\frac{1}{4}$

C) $\frac{1}{12}$

D) $\frac{1}{144}$

56

If $xy = 4$ and $x^2 + y^2 = 11$, then what is the value of $(3x - 3y)^2$?

A) 9

B) 24

C) 27

D) 63

57

$$a+\cfrac{1}{b+\cfrac{1}{c+\cfrac{1}{d}}}=\frac{71}{31}$$

Based on the operation given above, what is the value of $a + b + c + d$?

A) 3

B) 4

C) 9

D) 11

58

$$\frac{a^3b-ab^3}{a^2b-ab^2}=5$$

If $a-b=7$, then what is a^2-b^2?

A) 2
B) 12
C) 35
D) 70

59

If $a^2+ab+b^2=10$ and $a+ab+b=2$, then which of the following is equal to $a+b$?

A) -4
B) -3
C) 4
D) 7

60

$$\left(1-\frac{1}{2}\right)\cdot\left(1-\frac{1}{3}\right)\cdot\left(1-\frac{1}{4}\right)\cdots\cdots\cdots\left(1-\frac{1}{10}\right)$$

What is the result of the operation given above?

A) 0.1
B) 1
C) 9
D) 10

61

$$8-\cfrac{24}{5-\cfrac{12}{7-\cfrac{x+1}{6}}}=0$$

What is the value of x that satisfies the equation given above?

A) 2
B) 5
C) 11
D) 17

62

If $A=\frac{2}{7}+\frac{3}{11}+\frac{4}{13}$ and $B=\frac{5}{7}+\frac{19}{11}+\frac{35}{13}$, then what is $A+B$?

A) 2
B) 4
C) 6
D) 8

63

$$\left(1-\frac{1}{2}\right)\left(1+\frac{1}{3}\right)\left(1-\frac{1}{4}\right)\left(1+\frac{1}{5}\right)\cdots\left(1+\frac{1}{21}\right)$$

What is the value of the expression above?

A) $\frac{5}{21}$

B) $\frac{7}{21}$

C) $\frac{11}{21}$

D) $\frac{19}{21}$

64

$$A^2 = A + 1 \qquad A^5 = B + 1$$

What is the value of B?

A) 2A + 1

B) 3A + 2

C) 5A + 2

D) 5A + 3

65

If $\frac{1}{3}x = 4 - \frac{5}{6}y$, what is the value of $2x + 5y$?

66

$$\frac{x^2+6x}{x^2+6x-27}$$

What is the positive value of x that makes the expression above undefined?

67

$$x^2 = 6 + xy$$
$$y^2 = 3 + xy$$

Based on the expressions above what is the positive value of x-y ?

68

How many integer values of x are there if $\frac{2x+15}{x}$ is also an integer?

69

$$(x-6+y)^2+(x+2-y)^2=0$$

Given the equation above, find the value of $\frac{y}{x}$.

70

$$x^2-y^2=13$$

If $x<0$, $y>0$ and both x and y are integers, then find the value of $y-2x$.

71

$$a-\frac{3}{b}=5$$

$$b+\frac{7}{a}=5$$

Given the equations above, what is the value of $a-b$?

72

$a^2-2a-b^2+2b=27$ and $a-b=3$

If a and b are positive integers, then what is the value of a?

SECTION 2 - OPERATIONS w RATIONAL EXPRESSIONS

#	Answer	Topic	Subtopic	#	Answer	Topic	Subtopic	#	Answer	Topic	Subtopic	#	Answer	Topic	Subtopic
1	D	TB	S7	19	D	TB	S7	37	D	TB	S7	55	A	TB	S7
2	B	TB	S7	20	C	TB	S7	38	C	TB	S7	56	C	TB	S7
3	A	TB	S7	21	C	TB	S7	39	A	TB	S7	57	D	TB	S7
4	A	TB	S7	22	D	TB	S7	40	C	TB	S7	58	C	TB	S7
5	D	TB	S7	23	D	TB	S7	41	C	TB	S7	59	A	TB	S7
6	C	TB	S7	24	A	TB	S7	42	C	TB	S7	60	A	TB	S7
7	C	TB	S7	25	C	TB	S7	43	B	TB	S7	61	B	TB	S7
8	A	TB	S7	26	A	TB	S7	44	C	TB	S7	62	C	TB	S7
9	C	TB	S7	27	B	TB	S7	45	B	TB	S7	63	C	TB	S7
10	A	TB	S7	28	D	TB	S7	46	D	TB	S7	64	C	TB	S7
11	D	TB	S7	29	D	TB	S7	47	D	TB	S7	65	24	TB	S7
12	D	TB	S7	30	A	TB	S7	48	A	TB	S7	66	3	TB	S7
13	C	TB	S7	31	C	TB	S7	49	C	TB	S7	67	3	TB	S7
14	C	TB	S7	32	C	TB	S7	50	C	TB	S7	68	8	TB	S7
15	B	TB	S7	33	D	TB	S7	51	A	TB	S7	69	2	TB	S7
16	B	TB	S7	34	B	TB	S7	52	C	TB	S7	70	20	TB	S7
17	D	TB	S7	35	B	TB	S7	53	A	TB	S7	71	2	TB	S7
18	B	TB	S7	36	C	TB	S7	54	C	TB	S7	72	7	TB	S7

Topics & Subtopics

Code	Description	Code	Description
SB7	Operations with Rational Expressions	TB	Passport to Advanced Mathematics

CONTINUE ▶

1

$$\frac{1+10+100+1000}{0.001+0.01+0.1+1} = \frac{1111}{0.1111}$$

What is the value of the operation given above?

$$\frac{1111 \times 10{,}000}{0.1111 \times 10{,}000} = \frac{1111 \times 10{,}000}{1111} = 10{,}000$$

A) 10
B) 100
C) 1,000
D) 10,000

2

$$3(x - 2) + 2(x - 2) = -20$$

What is the value of $(x - 2)$?

$$\frac{5(x-2)}{5} = \frac{-20}{5}$$

$$(x-2) = -4$$

A) -6
B) -4
C) -3.6
D) -2

3

$$\left(2 - \frac{y}{y-1}\right) \div \frac{y-2}{5}$$

What is the simplified form of the equation above?

$$\frac{2y-2-y}{y-1} \cdot \frac{5}{y-2}$$

$$\frac{y-2}{y-1} \cdot \frac{5}{y-2} = \frac{5}{y-1}$$

A) $\frac{5}{y-1}$
B) $\frac{y-2}{y-1}$
C) $\frac{2y-1}{y-1}$
D) $\frac{1}{y-1}$

4

$$\frac{2x}{x+3} \div \frac{12}{3x+9}$$

Which of the following is equivalent to the expression above given that $x \neq -3$?

$$\frac{2x}{x+3} \cdot \frac{3(x+3)}{12} = \frac{6x}{12} = \frac{x}{2}$$

A) $\frac{x}{2}$
B) $2x$
C) $3x$
D) $8x$

5

$$3x - 2 = 8$$

What is the value of $12x + 8$?

$$4 \cdot (3x-2) = 8 \cdot 4$$

$$12x - 8 = 32$$

$$+8 \quad +8$$

$$12x = 40$$

$$+8 \quad +8$$

$$12x + 8 = 48$$

A) 24
B) 32
C) 40
D) 48

6

$$\frac{2 \cdot 3}{2 \cdot (x-2)} + \frac{5}{2x-4} = \frac{11}{12}$$

Based on the expression above, what is the value of $2x - 4$?

$$\frac{11}{2x-4} = \frac{11}{12}$$

$$2x - 4 = 12$$

$$+4 \quad +4$$

$$\frac{2x}{2} = \frac{16}{2} \qquad x = 8$$

A) 6
B) 8
C) 12
D) 16

CONTINUE ▶

7

$$\frac{0.004+0.04+0.4+4}{2+20+200+2000} = \frac{4.444}{2,222}$$

What is the value of the operation above?

A) 2　$\frac{4.444 \times 1,000}{2,222 \times 1,000} = \frac{4,444}{2,222 \times 1,000} = \frac{2}{1,000}$

B) 10^{-3}

C) 2.10^{-3}　$= 2 \times 10^{-3}$

D) 2000

8

$$\frac{1}{\dfrac{1}{x+1} + \dfrac{1}{x+2}}$$

Which of the following is equivalent to the expression above?

$\dfrac{1}{\dfrac{x+2+x+1}{(x+2)\cdot(x+1)}}$

A) $\dfrac{x^2+3x+2}{2x+3}$

B) $2x+3$

C) x^2+3x+2　$\dfrac{x^2+3x+2}{2x+3}$

D) $\dfrac{2x+3}{x^2+3x+2}$

9

The denominator of a fraction is 4 times its numerator. If 6 is added to both the numerator and denominator, then the value of the fraction is 0.5.　$\dfrac{x+6}{4x+6} = \dfrac{1}{2}$

What is the initial sum of the numerator and denominator of the fraction?

A) 5　$2x+12 = 4x+6$

$\quad\quad\;\; -2x-6 \quad -2x-6$

B) 10　$\dfrac{6}{2} = \dfrac{2x}{2}$　$3=x$

C) 15

$\quad x+4x = 5x = 5\cdot3 = 15$

D) 20

10

$$\frac{\dfrac{m}{n}}{5} \div \frac{m}{\dfrac{n}{5}}$$

If m and n are non zero integers, what is the value of the operation given above?

A) 0.04　$\left(\dfrac{m}{n} \cdot \dfrac{1}{5}\right) \div \left(\dfrac{m}{1} \cdot \dfrac{5}{n}\right)$

B) 1

C) 5　$\dfrac{m}{5n} \cdot \dfrac{n}{5m} = \dfrac{1}{25} = \dfrac{4}{100} = 0.04$

D) 25

11

$$\frac{4}{0.01}+\frac{0.4}{0.04}$$

What is the equivalent of the expression above?

$\dfrac{4 \times 100}{0.01 \times 100}+\dfrac{0.4 \times 100}{0.04 \times 100}$

A) 110

B) 114 $\dfrac{400}{1}+\dfrac{40}{4}=400+10=410$

C) 401

D) 410

12

If $x^2 - kx + 4$ is a perfect square, then what is the value of k^2? $\sqrt{4}=2$

A) -2   It must be $(x+2)^2$ or $(x-2)^2$

B) 2 x^2+4x+4 or x^2-4x+4

C) 4 $k=-4$ or $k=4$

D) 16 $k^2=16$

13

If $ab = \dfrac{1}{3}$, then what is the value of

$\left(a-\dfrac{1}{b}\right)\left(\dfrac{1}{a}-b\right)$? $\dfrac{ab}{1}=\dfrac{1}{3}$ $\dfrac{1}{ab}=\dfrac{3}{1}$

A) $-\dfrac{1}{3}$ $a\cdot\dfrac{1}{a}-ab-\dfrac{1}{ab}+b\cdot\dfrac{1}{b}$

B) -1

C) $-\dfrac{4}{3}$ $1-\dfrac{1}{3}-3+1$

D) $\dfrac{5}{3}$ $-1-\dfrac{1}{3}=\dfrac{-4}{3}$

14

$$\frac{a+b-1}{ab}=K$$

$$a=\frac{x}{x+y} \qquad b=\frac{y}{x+y}$$

What is the value of K?

$a+b=\dfrac{x}{x+y}+\dfrac{y}{x+y}=\dfrac{x+y}{x+y}=1$

A) -2

B) -1 $K=\dfrac{a+b-1}{ab}=\dfrac{1-1}{ab}=0$

C) 0

D) It can not be determined.

15

If $a = -2$ and $b = 2^{-1}$, then what is the value of $\dfrac{ab}{a^2+2b}$? $b=2^{-1}=\dfrac{1}{2}$

A) $-\dfrac{1}{2}$

B) $-\dfrac{1}{5}$ $\dfrac{ab}{a^2+2b}=\dfrac{-2\cdot\frac{1}{2}}{(-2)^2+2\cdot\frac{1}{2}}=\dfrac{-1}{5}$

C) $\dfrac{1}{5}$

D) 1

16

$$\frac{5(k+2)-4}{6} = \frac{8-(3-k)}{3}$$

What is the value of k in the equation above?

(handwritten work)
$$\frac{5(k+2)-4}{6} = \frac{8-(3-k)}{3}$$
$$\frac{5k+10-4}{6} = \frac{8-3+k}{3}$$
$$\frac{5k+6}{6} = \frac{(5+k)\cdot 2}{(3)\cdot 2}$$
$$\frac{5k+6}{6} = \frac{10+2k}{6}$$
$$5k+6 = 10+2k$$
$$-2k \quad -6 \qquad -6 \quad -2k$$
$$\frac{3k}{3} = \frac{4}{3}$$
$$k = \frac{4}{3}$$

A) $\dfrac{12}{21}$

B) $\dfrac{4}{3}$ *(circled)*

C) $\dfrac{3}{2}$

D) $\dfrac{16}{3}$

17

$$127^2 - 101^2 = 26k$$
$$x^2 - y^2 = (x+y)(x-y)$$

What is the value of k in the equation given above?

(handwritten work)
$$(127-101)\cdot(127+101) = 26k$$
$$26\cdot 228 = 26k$$
$$k = 228$$

A) 176

B) 187

C) 217

D) 228 *(circled)*

18

$$\frac{1-\dfrac{1}{x}}{1+\dfrac{1}{x}} = 3$$

What is the value of x?

(handwritten work)
$$\frac{\frac{x-1}{x}}{\frac{x+1}{x}} = \frac{x-1}{x}\cdot\frac{x}{x+1} = 3$$
$$\frac{x-1}{x+1} = 3$$
$$x-1 = 3x+3$$
$$-x-3 \quad -x-3$$
$$\frac{-4}{2} = \frac{2}{2}x \qquad x=-2$$

A) -3

B) -2 *(circled)*

C) -1

D) 1

19

$$a-b=b-c=4 \qquad a^2+c^2-2b^2 = K$$
$$a=4+b \qquad c=b-4$$

What is the value of K in the equation given above?

(handwritten work)
$$(4+b)^2 + (b-4)^2 - 2b^2 = K$$
$$16+8b+b^2+b^2-8b+16-2b^2 = K$$
$$32 = K$$

A) 16

B) 25

C) 28

D) 32 *(circled)*

20

$$\frac{x^2+5x-7}{x^3+3x^2-4x}$$

When denominator is zero, it is undefined

What values of x make the expression above undefined?

$x(x^2+3x-4) = x(x+4)(x-1)$
            ↓   ↓   ↓
            0 -4 1

A) 0,1,4

B) -4,1

C) -4,1,0

D) 4,0,-1

21

$$\frac{156^2+244^2+312\cdot 244}{2^3\cdot 5^3}$$

What is the value of the operation given above?

$\frac{(156+244)^2}{8\cdot 125} = \frac{400\cdot 400}{8\cdot 125}$

A) 16

B) 40

$= \frac{160,000}{1,000}$

C) 160

D) 400

$= 160$

22

$$\frac{x^2-7x+12}{8x+88x^2+240x}$$

Which of the following value of x makes the fraction above undefined?

A) $-\dfrac{30}{11}$ $88x^2+248x=0$

B) -4 $88x^2=-248x$

C) 3 $\frac{88x}{88}=\frac{-248}{88}$

D) $-\dfrac{31}{11}$ $x=-\frac{31}{11}$

23

$$(1003-105)(1003+105)+105^2 = A$$

$1003^2 - 1005^2 + 1005^2 = A$

What is the value of A?

$A = 1003^2$

A) 1003

B) 1108

C) 105^2

D) 1003^2

24

$$\frac{m}{n-1}+\left(\frac{m}{n-1}\right)^2+\left(\frac{m}{n-1}\right)^3$$

If $m+2n=2$, then what is the value of the operation given above?

$\frac{2n-2}{2}=\frac{-m}{2}$ $n-1=-\frac{m}{2}$

A) -6

$\frac{m}{n-1}=\frac{m}{-\frac{m}{2}}=m\cdot\frac{2}{-m}=-2$

B) -2

C) 8

D) 14 $-2+(-2)^2+(-2)^3=-2+4-8=-6$

25

$$\left(\frac{a}{b}+\frac{b}{a}\right)^2=(4)^2 \qquad \frac{a^2}{b^2}+\frac{b^2}{a^2}=K$$

What is the value of K?

$\frac{a^2}{b^2}+\frac{b^2}{a^2}+2\frac{a}{b}\cdot\frac{b}{a}=16$

A) 8

B) 12 $\frac{a^2}{b^2}+\frac{b^2}{a^2}+2=16$

C) 14 -2 -2

D) 16 $\frac{a^2}{b^2}+\frac{b^2}{a^2}=14$

CONTINUE ▶

26

The expression $\frac{3x-4}{x+2}$ is equivalent to which of the following ?

A) $3-\frac{10}{x+2}$

B) $3+\frac{2}{x+2}$

C) $3+\frac{10}{x+2}$

D) $3-\frac{2}{x+2}$

3
x+2) 3x − 4
− 3x + 6
−10

$\frac{3x-4}{x+2} = 3 + \frac{-10}{x+2}$

27

$$\frac{4y^2-100}{y+5}=12$$

What is the value of y?

A) -2

B) 8

C) 12

D) 17

$\frac{(2y-10)(2y+10)}{y+5} = 12$

$4y - 20 = 12$
$+20 \quad +20$

$\frac{4}{4}y = \frac{32}{4}$ $y = 8$

28

$$x^2 + y^2 = 49 - 2xy$$
$+2xy \qquad +2xy$

According to the equation given above, what is the positive value of $x + y$?

A) 4

B) 5

C) 6

D) 7

$x^2 + 2xy + y^2 = 49$

$(x+y)^2 = 7^2$

$x + y = 7$

29

$$a^2+ab=5$$
$$+\ b^2+ab=20$$

$a^2 + 2ab + b^2 = 25$

What is the positive value of $a+b$?

A) 2

B) 3

C) 4

D) 5

$(a+b)^2 = 25$

$a + b = 5$

30

$$\frac{6x+20}{x+2}=A+\frac{B}{x+2}$$

Based on the expression above, find A+B?

A) 14

B) 20

C) 26

D) 28

$\frac{6x+20}{x+2} = \frac{A(x+2)}{x+2} + \frac{B}{x+2}$

$6x + 20 = A(x+2) + B$

Set $x = -1$ to get A+B

$6 \cdot (-1) + 20 = A(-1+2) + B$

$14 = A + B$

31

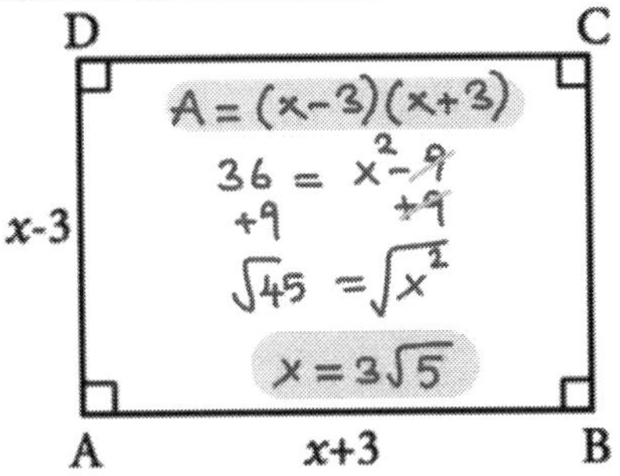

If the area of rectangle ABCD is 36, then what is the perimeter of ABCD?

A) 12
B) $6\sqrt{5}$
C) $12\sqrt{5}$
D) $12\sqrt{5}-6$

$P=2(x-3+x+3)$
$P=4x=4\cdot 3\sqrt{5}=12\sqrt{5}$

32

$$(444)^2-(333)^2=111^2\cdot k$$

$x^2-y^2=(x-y)(x+y)$

What is the value of k?

A) 1
B) 2
C) 7
D) 49

$(444-333)(444+333)=111^2\cdot k$
$111\cdot 777=111^2\cdot k$
$111\cdot 7\cdot 111=111^2\cdot k$
$7=k$

33

$$\frac{m-1}{m-3}=\frac{m-5}{m-4}$$

According to the equation above what is the value of m?

A) $\frac{8}{5}$
B) $\frac{13}{4}$
C) $\frac{9}{4}$
D) $\frac{11}{3}$

$(m-3)(m-5)=(m-1)(m-4)$
$m^2-8m+15=m^2-5m+4$
$+8m-4 \quad +8m-4$
$\frac{11}{3}=\frac{3}{3}m$
$m=\frac{11}{3}$

34

If $a-b=7$ and $ab=3$, then what is the value of $2a^2b^3-2a^3b^2$?

A) -252
B) -126
C) -84
D) 294

$2a^2b^2(b-a)=2(ab)^2\cdot-(a-b)$
$=2\cdot(3)^2\cdot -7$
$=2\cdot 9\cdot -7$
$=-126$

CONTINUE ▶

35

$$\frac{x(y+z)+z(y-x)}{x^2+xy+xz+yz}$$

What is the simplified form of the equation above?

A) $\frac{x}{x+y}$

B) $\frac{y}{x+y}$

C) $\frac{z}{x+z}$

D) $\frac{y}{y+z}$

36

$$\frac{1+\frac{1}{x}}{\frac{1}{x^2}-1}$$

What is the simplified form of the equation above?

A) $\frac{1}{x-1}$

B) $\frac{1}{1-x}$

C) $\frac{-x}{x-1}$

D) $\frac{x-1}{x}$

37

$$(x+4+y)^2+(x-8-y)^2=0$$

Given the equation above, what is the value of xy?

A) -6

B) 4

C) 2

D) -12

38

$$\frac{240^2-60^2}{80^2-20^2}$$

What is the simplified form of the equation given above?

A) 3

B) 6

C) 9

D) 12

CONTINUE ▶

39

$(18 - a)(18 + a) + 36 = 324$

$(x-y)(x+y) = x^2 + y^2$

What is the value of *a*?

$18^2 - a^2 + 36 = 324$

A) 6 $324 - a^2 + 36 = 324$

B) 36 $\quad -36 \quad\quad -36$

$\quad\quad -a^2 = -36$

C) 288 $\quad\quad a^2 = 36$

D) 360

$a = 6 \text{ or } -6$

40

$a + 3 = b + 4$

$\dfrac{1}{a+3} + \dfrac{1}{b+4} = 1 \quad \dfrac{1}{2} + \dfrac{1}{2} = 1$

Based on the equations above, what is the value of *a + b*?

$a + 3 = 2 \quad\quad b + 4 = 2$

A) -1 $-3 \quad -3 \quad\quad -4 \quad -4$

B) -2 $a = -1 \quad\quad b = -2$

C) -3

D) -4 $a + b = -1 + -2 = -3$

41

$x^2 - y^2 = 29$

$(x+y)(x-y) = 29$

If *x* and *y* are positive integers, then what is the value of *2x - y*?

$x + y = 29$

A) 14 $+ \; x - y = 1$

B) 15 $\dfrac{2x}{2} = \dfrac{30}{2}$

C) 16 $x = 15$

D) 30

$15 + y = 29$

$-15 \quad\quad -15$

$y = 14$

$2x - y = 2 \cdot 15 - 14$

$2x - y = 16$

42

If $x^2 + y^2 + 2x - 6y + 10 = 0$, then what is the value of *x + y*?

$x^2 + 2x + 1 + y^2 - 6y + 9 + 10 = 0 + 1 + 9$

$\quad\quad\quad\quad\quad\quad\quad -10 \quad -10$

A) -1

B) -2 $(x+1)^2 + (y-3)^2 = 0$

C) 2 $x = -1 \quad y = 3$

D) 4 $x + y = -1 + 3 = 2$

43

$(x+2)^2 + y^2 + 9 = 6y$

$\quad\quad\quad\quad -6y \quad -6y$

What is the sum of the values of *x* and *y* that satisfy the equation given above?

$(x+2)^2 + y^2 - 6y + 9 = 0$

A) -1 $(x+2)^2 + (y-3)^2 = 0$

B) 1 $x + 2 = 0 \quad\quad y - 3 = 0$

C) 5 $-2 \; -2 \quad\quad +3 \; +3$

D) 6 $x = -2 \quad\quad y = 3$

$x + y = -2 + 3 = 1$

44

$\dfrac{5}{2x+1} + \dfrac{2x+1}{5} = \dfrac{17}{5} + \dfrac{5}{17}$

What is the value of *x* that satisfies the equation given above?

$2x + 1 = 17$

$\quad\quad -1 \quad -1$

A) 5

B) 7 $\dfrac{2x}{2} = \dfrac{16}{2}$

C) 8

D) 9 $x = 8$

45

$$\frac{x}{y} = \frac{y}{z} \qquad x^2 + xz + 2xy = 4$$

$$xz = y^2$$

Based on the equations given above, what is the value of $x + y$?

$$x^2 + y^2 + 2xy = 4$$

A) 1

$$(x+y)^2 = 4$$

B) 2

C) 4

$$x+y = 2 \quad \text{or} \quad x+y = -2$$

D) 16

46

$$x^2 + y^2 - 6x + 8y + 69$$

What is the minimum value of the expression given above if both x and y are integers?

$$x^2 - 6x + 9 + y^2 + 8y + 16 + 44$$

A) 36

$$(x-3)^2 + (y+4)^2 + 44$$

B) 39   when $x=3$, $y=-4$ it gets the

C) 42   minimum value.

D) 44 $(3-3)^2 + (-4+4)^2 + 44 = 44$

47

$$\left[\left(\frac{1}{x} + \frac{1}{y}\right)^2 - \left(\frac{1}{x} - \frac{1}{y}\right)^2\right] \cdot xy$$

$$a^2 - b^2 = (a+b)(a-b)$$

What is the result of the operation given above?

$$\left(\frac{1}{x} + \frac{1}{y} + \frac{1}{x} - \frac{1}{y}\right)\left(\frac{1}{x} + \frac{1}{y} - \frac{1}{x} + \frac{1}{y}\right) \cdot xy$$

A) -1

B) 0 $\dfrac{2}{x} \cdot \dfrac{2}{y} \cdot xy = 4$

C) 1

D) 4

48

$$xy = 2 \qquad (x+y)^2 = (4)^2$$

$$\frac{x \cdot x}{x \cdot y} + \frac{y \cdot y}{x \cdot y} = M$$

$$M = \frac{x^2 + y^2}{xy}$$

What is the value of M?

$$x^2 + y^2 + 2xy = 16 \qquad x^2 + y^2 + 2 \cdot 2 = 16$$

A) 6

$$x^2 + y^2 = 12$$

B) 8

C) 10 $M = \dfrac{x^2 + y^2}{xy} = \dfrac{12}{2} = 6$

D) 12

49

$$2x - y = 4 \qquad 3a + b = 5$$

According to the equations given above, what is the value of $6ax + 2bx - 3ay - yb$?

$$6ax - 3ay + 2bx - yb$$

A) 1

$$3a(2x - y) + b(2x - y)$$

B) 9

C) 20 $(2x - y) \cdot (3a + b)$

D) 40 $4 \cdot 5 = 20$

53

CONTINUE ▶

50

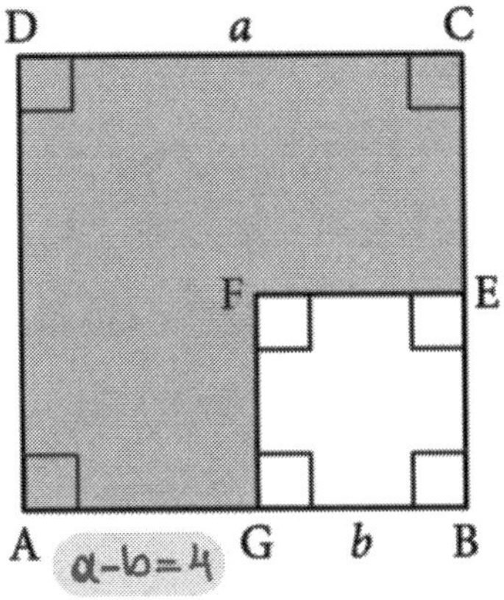

ABCD and GBEF are squares. If the shaded area is $40cm^2$ and AG=4cm, then what is the value of a? $a^2-b^2=(a+b)(a-b)$

A) 4 $\frac{40}{4}=(a+b)\cdot\frac{4}{4}$ $a+b=10$

B) 6 $a+b=10$

C) 7 $+\ a-b=4$

D) 10 $\frac{2a}{2}=\frac{14}{2}$ $a=7$

51

$$\frac{a-b}{a+b}=\frac{3}{7}$$

$7a-7b=3a+3b$ $4a=10b$

Based on the equation above, find the value of $\frac{a^2+b^2}{a^2-b^2}$. Let $a=10$, $b=4$ then:

A) $\frac{29}{21}$ $\frac{a^2+b^2}{a^2-b^2}=\frac{10^2+4^2}{10^2-4^2}=\frac{116}{84}=\frac{29}{21}$

B) $\frac{28}{27}$

C) $\frac{15}{17}$

D) $\frac{21}{25}$

52

$$\frac{2\cdot 5x}{2\cdot(x-3)}+\frac{2x}{2x-6}=\frac{54}{3x-9}$$

What value of x satisfies the equation given above? $\frac{10x+2x}{2(x-3)}=\frac{54}{3(x-3)}$

A) 3 $6x=18$ $x=3$

B) 6 But denominator can NOT be zero. So, there is no solution.

C) There is no solution.

D) There are infinitely many solutions.

53

If $a^2 - a = b^2 - b$, and $ab = -1$, then what is the value of $a^2 + b^2$?

A) 3

B) 4

C) 5

D) 6

$a^2-a=b^2-b$

$-b^2+a \quad -b^2+a$

$a^2-b^2=a-b$

$(a+b)(a-b)=a-b$ $a+b=1$

$(a+b)^2=a^2+2ab+b^2$

$1^2=a^2+2(-1)+b^2$

$1=a^2+b^2-2$

$+2 \quad +2$

$a^2+b^2=3$

54

$$\frac{a^2-(b-1)^2}{a+b-1}=17$$

What is the value of *a* - *b*?

$$\frac{(a+b-1)(a-b+1)}{a+b-1}=17$$

$a-b+1=17$

$a-b=16$

A) 13
B) 15
C) 16
D) 18

55

$$(a-b)^2+4ab$$

$a^2-2ab+b^2+4ab=a^2+2ab+b^2=(a+b)^2$

Find the value of the expression above for $a=\frac{11}{24}$ and $b=\frac{13}{24}$.

A) 1 $\quad (a+b)^2=\left(\frac{11}{24}+\frac{13}{24}\right)^2=\left(\frac{24}{24}\right)^2=1$

B) $\frac{1}{4}$

C) $\frac{1}{12}$

D) $\frac{1}{144}$

56

If $xy = 4$ and $x^2 + y^2 = 11$, then what is the value of $(3x - 3y)^2$?

$(3x-3y)^2=3^2(x-y)^2=9(x^2-2xy+y^2)$
$=9(11-2\cdot 4)$
$=9\cdot 3$
$=27$

A) 9
B) 24
C) 27
D) 63

57

$$a+\cfrac{1}{b+\cfrac{1}{c+\cfrac{1}{d}}}=\frac{71}{31}=2+\frac{9}{31}$$

$a=2$

Based on the operation given above, what is the value of $a + b + c + d$?

$2+\frac{9}{31}=2+\frac{1}{\frac{31}{9}}\rightarrow 3+\frac{4}{9}$ $\quad b=3$

$3+\frac{4}{9}=3+\frac{1}{\frac{9}{4}}\rightarrow 2+\frac{1}{4}$ $\quad c=2$, $d=4$

A) 3
B) 4
C) 9
D) 11 $\quad a+b+c+d=2+3+2+4=11$

58

$$\frac{a^3b-ab^3}{a^2b-ab^2}=5 = \frac{ab(a^2-b^2)}{ab(a-b)}$$

If $a-b=7$, then what is a^2-b^2?

$\frac{(a+b)(a-b)}{(a-b)}=5$

A) 2
B) 12
C) 35 $a^2-b^2=(a+b)(a-b)=5\cdot 7=35$
D) 70

59

If $a^2+ab+b^2=10$ and $a+ab+b=2$, then which of the following is equal to $a+b$?

$a^2+ab+b^2=10$
$+\ a+ab+b=2$
$a^2+2ab+b^2+a+b=12$
$(a+b)^2+(a+b)=12$

A) -4
B) -3
C) 4
D) 7

After this step try options.
−4 works
or; let $a+b=x$ and solve it.

60

$$\left(1-\frac{1}{2}\right)\cdot\left(1-\frac{1}{3}\right)\cdot\left(1-\frac{1}{4}\right)\cdots\cdots\cdots\left(1-\frac{1}{10}\right)$$

What is the result of the operation given above?

$\frac{1}{2}\cdot\frac{2}{3}\cdot\frac{3}{4}\cdots\cdots\frac{9}{10}=\frac{1}{10}=0.1$

A) 0.1
B) 1
C) 9
D) 10

61

$$8-\cfrac{24}{5-\cfrac{12}{7-\cfrac{x+1}{6}}}=0$$

This part must be 8. This part must be 3.

What is the value of x that satisfies the equation given above?

$5-\frac{12}{7-\frac{x+1}{6}}=3$ (This must be 2)

$\frac{12}{7-\frac{x+1}{6}}=2$ (Must be 6)

$7-\frac{x+1}{6}=6$ (Must be 1)

$\frac{x+1}{6}=1$ $x=5$

A) 2
B) 5
C) 11
D) 17

62

If $A=\frac{2}{7}+\frac{3}{11}+\frac{4}{13}$ and $B=\frac{5}{7}+\frac{19}{11}+\frac{35}{13}$, then what is $A+B$?

$B=1-\frac{2}{7}+2-\frac{3}{11}+3-\frac{4}{13}$

$B=6-\left(\frac{2}{7}+\frac{3}{11}+\frac{4}{13}\right)$

$B=6-A$

$A+B=A+6-A=6$

A) 2
B) 4
C) 6
D) 8

CONTINUE ▶

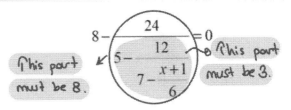

63

$$\left(1-\frac{1}{2}\right)\left(1+\frac{1}{3}\right)\left(1-\frac{1}{4}\right)\left(1+\frac{1}{5}\right)\cdots\left(1+\frac{1}{21}\right)$$

What is the value of the expression above?

A) $\frac{5}{21}$ $\frac{1}{2}\cdot\frac{4}{3}\cdot\frac{3}{4}\cdot\frac{6}{5}\cdot\frac{5}{6}\cdots\frac{19}{20}\cdot\frac{22}{21}$

B) $\frac{7}{21}$ $\frac{1}{2}\cdot\frac{22}{21}=\frac{11}{21}$

C) $\frac{11}{21}$

D) $\frac{19}{21}$

64

$$A^2 = A+1 \qquad A^5 = B+1$$

$A^2 \cdot A^2 \cdot A = B+1$

What is the value of B?

$(A+1)(A+1)A = B+1$

A) $2A+1$ $(A^2+2A+1)\cdot A = B+1$

B) $3A+2$ $(A+1+2A+1)\cdot A = B+1$

C) $5A+2$ $(3A+2)A = B+1$

D) $5A+3$ $3A^2+2A = B+1$

$3(A+1)+2A = B+1$

$5A+3 = B+1$

$-1 \quad -1$

$B = 5A+2$

65

If $\frac{1}{3}x = 4-\frac{5}{6}y$, what is the value of $2x+5y$?

$6\cdot\frac{1}{3}x = 6\cdot 4 - \frac{6\cdot 5}{6}y$ $2x = 24-5y$

$+5y \quad +5y$

$2x+5y=24$

66

$$\frac{x^2+6x}{x^2+6x-27}$$ $(x+9)(x-3)$

$x=-9$ $x=3$

What is the positive value of x that makes the expression above undefined?

$x=3$ makes it undefined

67

$$x^2 = 6+xy$$
$$+ \quad y^2 = 3+xy$$
$$x^2+y^2 = 9+2xy$$
$$-2xy \quad -2xy$$

Based on the expressions above what is the positive value of x-y?

$x^2-2xy+y^2=9$ $(x-y)^2=9$ $x-y=3$

68

How many integer values of x are there if $\frac{2x+15}{x}$ is also an integer?

$\frac{2x}{x}+\frac{15}{x}$ $x \rightarrow 1, 3, 5, 15$

$-1, -3, -5, -15$

X can take 8 different values so, there are 8 integer values.

CONTINUE ▶

69

$$(x-6+y)^2+(x+2-y)^2=0$$

$x-6+y=0$ $x+2-y=0$
$+6$ $+6$ -2 -2

Given the equation above, find the value of $\frac{y}{x}$.

$x+y=6$
$+\ x-y=-2$
$\frac{2x}{2}=\frac{4}{2}$ $x=2$

$2+y=6$
-2 -2
$y=4$

$\frac{y}{x}=\frac{4}{2}=2$

70

$$x^2-y^2=13$$

$(x+y)(x-y)=13$

If $x<0,\ y>0$ and both x and y are integers, then find the value of $y-2x$.

Factors of 13 are -13 and -1;

$x+y=-1$
$+\ x-y=-13$
$\frac{2x}{2}=\frac{-14}{2}$
$x=-7$

$-7+y=-1$
$+7$ $+7$
$y=6$

$y-2x=6-2(-7)=20$

71

$a-\frac{3}{b}=5$ $ab-3=5b$

$b+\frac{7}{a}=5$ $ab+7=5a$

Given the equations above, what is the value of $a-b$?

$-ab+3=-5b$
$+\ ab+7=5a$
$\frac{10}{5}=\frac{5(a-b)}{5}$ $a-b=2$

72

$a^2-2a-b^2+2b=27$ and $a-b=3$

$a^2-b^2-2(a-b)=27$

If a and b are positive integers, then what is the value of a?

$a^2-b^2-2\cdot 3=27$
$a^2-b^2-6=27$
$+6$ $+6$
$a^2-b^2=33$

$a^2-b^2=(a+b)(a-b)$
$\frac{33}{3}=(a+b)\cdot\frac{3}{3}$
$a+b=11$

$a+b=11$
$+\ a-b=3$
$\frac{2a}{2}=\frac{14}{2}$ $a=7$

CONTINUE ▶

Math Test – Calculator

DIRECTIONS

For multiple choice questions, choose the best answers from the choices after you solve the questions. Check your answers from the answer key.

For free responce questions, find your answer, write it in the space provided below and finally check it from the answer key.

NOTES

1. Calculator **is allowed**.
2. All variables are real numbers unless otherwise indicated.
3. Figures of this test are drawn to scale unless otherwise indicated.
4. Figures of this test lie in a plane.
5. Unless otherwise stated, the domain of function *f* is the set of all real numbers *x* for which *f(x)* is a real number.

REFERENCE

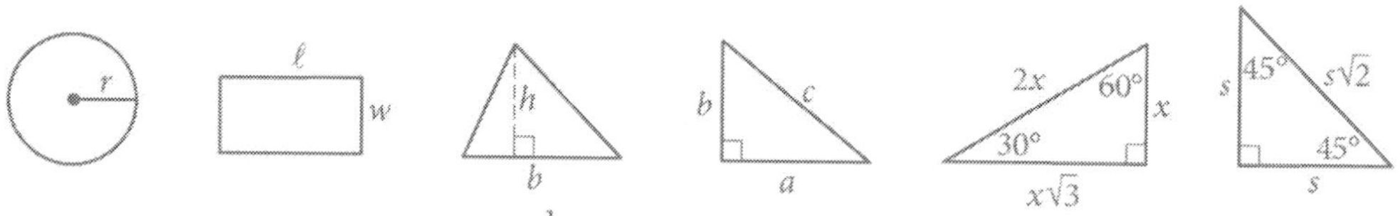

$A = \pi r^2$ $C = 2\pi r$ | $A = \ell w$ | $A = \frac{1}{2}bh$ | $c^2 = a^2 + b^2$ | Special Right Triangles

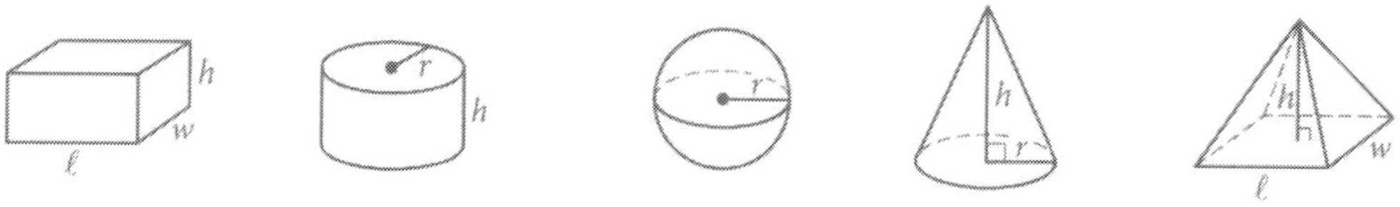

$V = \ell wh$ | $V = \pi r^2 h$ | $V = \frac{4}{3}\pi r^3$ | $V = \frac{1}{3}\pi r^2 h$ | $V = \frac{1}{3}\ell wh$

The number of degrees of a circle is 360.

The number of radians of a circle is 2π.

The sum of the angles of a triangle is 180 degrees.

1

$$\frac{\sqrt{12,1}-\sqrt{10}}{\sqrt{0,9}}$$

What is the result of the operation given above?

A) 0.20
B) 0.33
C) 0.50
D) 0.75

2

$$\sqrt[3]{9^{x-2}}=81$$

What is the value of x in the equation given above?

A) 1
B) 2
C) 4
D) 8

3

$$\frac{\sqrt{108}+\sqrt{12}}{\sqrt{48}}$$

What is the result of the operation above?

A) $\sqrt{3}$
B) $3\sqrt{3}$
C) $2\sqrt{3}$
D) 2

4

$$\frac{\sqrt{12}+\sqrt{75}}{\sqrt{27}-\sqrt{3}}$$

What is the result of the operation given above?

A) 2
B) 2.5
C) 3
D) 3.5

5

$$2(x-4)^2-m=0$$
$$x_1=4+\sqrt{5}$$

An equation and one of its roots is given above. What is the value of m?

A) 5
B) 10
C) 20
D) 50

6

$$\frac{\sqrt{n}}{4}=3\sqrt{2}$$

What is the value of n in the equation given above?

A) 24
B) 72
C) 288
D) 576

7

$$(x+1)^2 = 4 \qquad (x-1)^2 = 16$$

What is the value of x that satisfies the equations given above?

A) -3
B) -1
C) 1
D) 3

8

$$\frac{\sqrt{0.36}+\sqrt{1.21}-\sqrt{1.69}}{0.2}$$

What is the result of the operation given above?

A) 0.75
B) 2
C) 2.5
D) 4

9

$$\frac{3\sqrt{5}}{m}+\frac{1}{2\sqrt{5}}=\frac{3\sqrt{5}}{5}$$

What is the value of m?

A) 1.5
B) 3
C) 6
D) 30

10

If $a = b^{-\frac{1}{5}}$, where $a > 0$ and $b > 0$, then find b in terms of a ?

A) $b = \frac{1}{a^5}$
B) $b = -5a$
C) $b = \sqrt[5]{a}$
D) $b = -a^5$

11

$$\sqrt{\frac{1}{9}+\frac{1}{16}}$$

What is the result of the operation given above?

A) 0.143
B) 0.286
C) 0.417
D) 0.583

12

$$\frac{\sqrt{a}.\sqrt[8]{a^6}}{\sqrt[4]{a}}$$

What is the equivalent of the expression above?

A) a
B) a^2
C) $\sqrt[4]{a}$
D) $\sqrt[8]{a}$

13

$$\sqrt{1+\frac{5}{4}}-\sqrt{2-\frac{14}{25}}+\sqrt{1+\frac{36}{64}}=A$$

Based on the expression above what is the value of A?

A) $\frac{31}{20}$

B) $\frac{3}{2}$

C) 1

D) $\frac{21}{5}$

14

$$\left(2\sqrt{0,09}+4\sqrt[3]{0,027}\right)\cdot\frac{1}{9}$$

What is the result of the operation given above?

A) $\frac{1}{5}$

B) $\frac{1}{3}$

C) $\frac{9}{5}$

D) $\frac{10}{3}$

15

$$\sqrt{4}-\sqrt[3]{-8}+\sqrt{(-2)^4}\div\sqrt[4]{(-4)^2}$$

What is the result of the operation given above?

A) 2

B) 3

C) 4

D) 6

16

$$\sqrt{2+\sqrt[4]{14-\sqrt[3]{-8}}}$$

What is the result of the operation given above?

A) 0

B) 1

C) 2

D) 4

17

$$m=\sqrt{9m+7}-3$$

What is the sum of all solutions to the equation above?

A) 1
B) 2
C) 3
D) 4

18

$$a=\sqrt{2}$$
$$b=\sqrt{7}$$
$$c=\sqrt{56}$$

What is the value of $\frac{c}{a^3b}$?

A) 1
B) 2
C) 7
D) $\sqrt{2}$

19

$$m=\sqrt{12}-\sqrt{8}$$
$$n=\sqrt{27}+\sqrt{18}$$

Based on the expressions given above, what is the value of mn?

A) 6
B) 12
C) 18
D) 30

20

$$\sqrt{\frac{4^7+4^7+4^7+4^7}{2^6+2^6+2^6+2^6}}=A$$

According to the equation above what is the value of A?

A) 2
B) 4
C) 16
D) 64

21

$$\frac{\sqrt[4]{(-3)^4}-\sqrt{(-5)^2}}{\sqrt[5]{(-0.2)^5}}$$

What is the value of the operation given above?

A) - 40
B) - 10
C) 4
D) 10

22

$$a = \sqrt{3} + 1$$
$$b = \sqrt{3} - 1$$

What is the equivalent of $\frac{a+b}{a \cdot b}$?

A) $\sqrt{3}$
B) $\frac{\sqrt{3}}{3}$
C) $\frac{1}{3}$
D) $\frac{1}{4}$

23

$$\left(\sqrt{m} \cdot \sqrt[4]{m}\right)^2$$

If $m = 4$, what is the value of the operation given above?

A) 2
B) 4
C) 8
D) 16

24

$$\sqrt[4]{(-3)^4} + \sqrt[3]{(-2)^3} + \sqrt[6]{(-4)^6}$$

What is the value of the operation given above?

A) -7
B) -6
C) 5
D) 9

25

$$\sqrt[3]{(-8)^2} + \sqrt[3]{-3^3} + \sqrt{(-6)^2}$$

What is the result of the operation given above?

A) -1
B) 6
C) 7
D) 9

26

$$x - 5 = \sqrt{4x + 1}$$

Based on the equation above what is the value of x?

A) 2
B) 12
C) 2 or 12
D) None of the above

27

$$x - \sqrt{2x} = 4$$

Based on the equation above, what is the value of x?

A) 6
B) 8
C) 9
D) 12

28

If $a=\sqrt{2}+1$, what is the equivalent of $a(a-1)(a-2)$?

A) $-\sqrt{2}$
B) 1
C) $\sqrt{2}$
D) $3+\sqrt{2}$

29

$$\frac{\sqrt{\frac{7}{9}-\frac{3}{4}}}{\sqrt{\frac{4}{9}-\frac{7}{16}}}$$

What is the result of the operation given above?

A) 0.5
B) 1
C) 2
D) 4

30

$$a+b=\sqrt{7}$$
$$b-c=\sqrt{5}$$

What is the value of $b^2-bc+ab-ac$?

A) $\sqrt{2}$
B) $\sqrt{35}$
C) $\sqrt{7}-\sqrt{5}$
D) 2

31

$$a=\sqrt{6}+1$$
$$b=\sqrt{6}-1$$

What is the equivalent of $\frac{a}{b}+\frac{b}{a}$?

A) 2
B) 3
C) $\frac{4}{5}$
D) $\frac{14}{5}$

32

$$\sqrt[4]{4^8+\frac{4^8-4^{10}}{2^4}}$$

What is the result of the operation given above?

A) 4
B) 8
C) 16
D) 32

33

$$a=\sqrt{2}+\sqrt{24}$$
$$b=\sqrt{6}+\sqrt{20}$$
$$c=\sqrt{8}+\sqrt{18}$$

Which of the following order is correct about $a, b,$ and c given above?

A) $b=a=c$
B) $a<b<c$
C) $b<c=a$
D) $c<a<b$

34

$$\sqrt[x]{a}\cdot\sqrt[y]{a}$$

What is the equivalent of the expression above?

A) $\sqrt[xy]{a}$
B) $\sqrt[xy]{a^2}$
C) $\sqrt[x+y]{a^{xy}}$
D) $\sqrt[xy]{a^{x+y}}$

35

$$\sqrt{3-\sqrt{7}}\cdot\sqrt{3+\sqrt{5}}\cdot\sqrt{3+\sqrt{7}}\cdot\sqrt{3-\sqrt{5}}$$

What is the result of the operation given above?

A) 2
B) $2\sqrt{2}$
C) 4
D) 8

36

$$\frac{\sqrt{x-3}+\sqrt{3-x}+4x}{x-1}=A$$

If A is a real number, what is the value of A?

A) 3
B) 4
C) 6
D) 12

37

$$\mathrm{A}=\left(\sqrt{2}-\sqrt{3}+1\right)^2\cdot\left(\sqrt{2}+\sqrt{3}+1\right)^2$$

What is the value of A?

A) $\sqrt{2}+1$
B) $4+4\sqrt{2}$
C) $4\sqrt{2}$
D) 8

38

$$\sqrt{2x+9}-\sqrt{17-3x}$$

For how many integer values of x is the operation above defined in real numbers?

A) 10
B) 11
C) 12
D) 13

CONTINUE ▶

39

If $m=\sqrt{3}-1$ and $n=\sqrt{3}+1$ what is $\frac{m}{n}-\frac{n}{m}$?

A) $\sqrt{3}$
B) $-\sqrt{3}$
C) $-2\sqrt{3}$
D) -1

40

$$f(m)=\sqrt{m^2+16}$$

Which of the following values of x is not in the range of $f(m)$?

A) 3
B) 4
C) 5
D) 6

41

$$mn=144$$

$$\frac{1}{\sqrt{m}}+\frac{1}{\sqrt{n}}=\frac{7}{12}$$

What is the value of $m+n$ in the equation given above?

A) 7
B) 9
C) 16
D) 25

42

$$\sqrt{2019\cdot 2015+4}$$

What is the value of the operation given above?

A) 2013
B) 2015
C) 2017
D) 2019

43

$$a = \sqrt{2}$$
$$b = \sqrt{6}$$
$$c = \sqrt{10}$$

What is the value of $\sqrt{15}$ in terms of $a, b,$ and c?

A) $\frac{a^2 b}{c}$
B) $\frac{ac^2}{b}$
C) $\frac{bc}{a^2}$
D) $\frac{a+b}{c}$

44

The sum of the square root of two integers is 7. If the square root of the sum of the integers is 5, then what is the product of these integers?

A) 9
B) 16
C) 64
D) 144

45

$$\frac{\sqrt{x}}{3} = 2\sqrt{5}$$

What is the value of x in the equation given above?

46

$$m = 3\sqrt{2} \qquad 4m = \sqrt{2x}$$

What is the value of x in the equation given above?

47

$$\frac{\sqrt{n}}{4\sqrt{3}} = 2$$

What is the value of n in the equation given above?

48

$$A = \frac{2}{\sqrt{3}-2} - \frac{2}{\sqrt{3}+2}$$

What is the value of A^2?

CONTINUE ▶

49

The sum of an integer and three times its square root is 40. What is the square root of the integer?

50

The square root of a positive number is the same as the number divided by 20. What is the square root of that number?

51

$$\frac{n}{6\sqrt{5}} - \frac{2\sqrt{5}}{3} = \frac{2}{\sqrt{5}}$$

What is the value of *n* in the equation given above?

52

$$\sqrt{7-\sqrt{13}} \cdot \sqrt{7+\sqrt{13}}$$

What is the value of the radical equation given above?

SECTION 3 - RADICALS & RADICAL EQUATIONS

#	Answer	Topic	Subtopic
1	B	TB	S6
2	D	TB	S6
3	D	TB	S6
4	D	TB	S6
5	B	TB	S6
6	C	TB	S6
7	A	TB	S6
8	B	TB	S6
9	C	TB	S6
10	A	TB	S6
11	C	TB	S6
12	A	TB	S6
13	A	TB	S6

#	Answer	Topic	Subtopic
14	A	TB	S6
15	D	TB	S6
16	C	TB	S6
17	C	TB	S6
18	A	TB	S6
19	A	TB	S6
20	C	TB	S6
21	D	TB	S6
22	A	TB	S6
23	C	TB	S6
24	C	TB	S6
25	C	TB	S6
26	B	TB	S6

#	Answer	Topic	Subtopic
27	B	TB	S6
28	C	TB	S6
29	C	TB	S6
30	B	TB	S6
31	D	TB	S6
32	B	TB	S6
33	B	TB	S6
34	D	TB	S6
35	B	TB	S6
36	C	TB	S6
37	D	TB	S6
38	A	TB	S6
39	C	TB	S6

#	Answer	Topic	Subtopic
40	A	TB	S6
41	D	TB	S6
42	C	TB	S6
43	C	TB	S6
44	D	TB	S6
45	180	TB	S6
46	144	TB	S6
47	192	TB	S6
48	64	TB	S6
49	5	TB	S6
50	20	TB	S6
51	32	TB	S6
52	6	TB	S6

Topics & Subtopics

Code	Description
SB6	Radicals & Radical Equations

Code	Description
TB	Passport to Advanced Mathematics

CONTINUE ▶

1

$$\frac{\sqrt{12{,}1}-\sqrt{10}}{\sqrt{0{,}9}}$$

What is the result of the operation given above?

$$\frac{\sqrt{\frac{121}{10}}-\sqrt{\frac{100}{10}}}{\sqrt{\frac{9}{10}}}=\frac{\frac{11}{\sqrt{10}}-\frac{10}{\sqrt{10}}}{\frac{3}{\sqrt{10}}}=\frac{1}{\sqrt{10}}\cdot\frac{\sqrt{10}}{3}=\frac{1}{3}=0.33$$

A) 0.20
B) 0.33
C) 0.50
D) 0.75

2

$$\sqrt[3]{9^{x-2}}=81$$

What is the value of x in the equation given above?

$$9^{\frac{x-2}{3}}=9^{2}$$
$$3\cdot\frac{x-2}{3}=2\cdot 3$$
$$x-2=6 \quad +2 \quad +2 \qquad x=8$$

A) 1
B) 2
C) 4
D) 8

3

$$\frac{\sqrt{108}+\sqrt{12}}{\sqrt{48}}$$

What is the result of the operation above?

$$\frac{\sqrt{36\cdot 3}+\sqrt{4\cdot 3}}{\sqrt{16\cdot 3}}=\frac{6\sqrt{3}+2\sqrt{3}}{4\sqrt{3}}=\frac{8\sqrt{3}}{4\sqrt{3}}=2$$

A) $\sqrt{3}$
B) $3\sqrt{3}$
C) $2\sqrt{3}$
D) 2

4

$$\frac{\sqrt{12}+\sqrt{75}}{\sqrt{27}-\sqrt{3}}$$

What is the result of the operation given above?

$$\frac{\sqrt{3}\cdot\sqrt{4}+\sqrt{3}\cdot\sqrt{25}}{\sqrt{3}\cdot\sqrt{9}-\sqrt{3}\cdot 1}=\frac{\sqrt{3}\,(\sqrt{4}+\sqrt{25})}{\sqrt{3}\,(\sqrt{9}-1)}=\frac{2+5}{3-1}=\frac{7}{2}=3.5$$

A) 2
B) 2.5
C) 3
D) 3.5

5

$$2(x-4)^2-m=0$$
$$x_1=4+\sqrt{5}$$

An equation and one of its roots is given above. What is the value of m?

$$2(4+\sqrt{5}-4)^2-m=0 \quad +m \quad +m$$
$$2\cdot 5=m$$
$$10=m$$

A) 5
B) 10
C) 20
D) 50

6

$$4\cdot\frac{\sqrt{n}}{4}=3\sqrt{2}\cdot 4$$

What is the value of n in the equation given above?

$$(\sqrt{n})^2=(12\sqrt{2})^2$$
$$n=144\cdot 2$$
$$n=288$$

A) 24
B) 72
C) 288
D) 576

CONTINUE ▶

7

$$(x+1)^2 = 4 \qquad (x-1)^2 = 16$$

What is the value of x that satisfies the equations given above?

When you try the options -3 works.
There is no need to solve for x.

A) -3
B) -1
C) 1
D) 3

8

$$\frac{\sqrt{0.36}+\sqrt{1.21}-\sqrt{1.69}}{0.2}$$

What is the result of the operation given above?

$$\frac{\sqrt{\frac{36}{100}}+\sqrt{\frac{121}{100}}-\sqrt{\frac{169}{100}}}{0.2}$$

$$\frac{0.6+1.1-1.3}{0.2}=\frac{0.4}{0.2}=2$$

A) 0.75
B) 2
C) 2.5
D) 4

9

$$\frac{3\sqrt{5}}{m}+\frac{1}{2\sqrt{5}}=\frac{3\sqrt{5}}{5}$$

$$-\frac{1}{2\sqrt{5}} \qquad -\frac{1}{2\sqrt{5}}$$

What is the value of m?

$$\frac{3\sqrt{5}}{m}=\frac{3\sqrt{5}\cdot 2}{5\cdot 2}-\frac{1\cdot\sqrt{5}}{2\sqrt{5}\cdot\sqrt{5}}$$

$$\frac{3\sqrt{5}}{m}=\frac{6\sqrt{5}-\sqrt{5}}{10} \qquad \frac{3\sqrt{5}}{m}=\frac{5\sqrt{5}}{10}$$

$$\frac{3\cdot 10}{5}=\frac{5m}{5}$$

$m=6$

A) 1.5
B) 3
C) 6
D) 30

10

If $a = b^{-\frac{1}{5}}$, where $a>0$ and $b>0$, then find b in terms of a?

$$(a)^{-5}=\left(b^{-\frac{1}{5}}\right)^{-5}$$

$$\frac{1}{a^5}=b$$

A) $b=\frac{1}{a^5}$
B) $b=-5a$
C) $b=\sqrt[5]{a}$
D) $b=-a^5$

11

$$\sqrt{\frac{1}{9}+\frac{1}{16}}$$

What is the result of the operation given above?

$$\sqrt{\frac{1\cdot 16}{9\cdot 16}+\frac{1\cdot 9}{16\cdot 9}}=\sqrt{\frac{25}{144}}$$

$$=\frac{5}{12}$$

$$=0.417$$

A) 0.143
B) 0.286
C) 0.417
D) 0.583

12

$$\frac{\sqrt{a}.\sqrt[8]{a^6}}{\sqrt[4]{a}}$$

What is the equivalent of the expression above?

$$\frac{a^{\frac{1}{2}}\cdot a^{\frac{6}{8}}}{a^{\frac{1}{4}}}=a^{\frac{1\cdot 4}{2\cdot 4}+\frac{6}{8}-\frac{1\cdot 2}{4\cdot 2}}$$

$$=a^{\frac{8}{8}}=a^1=a$$

A) a
B) a^2
C) $\sqrt[4]{a}$
D) $\sqrt[8]{a}$

CONTINUE ▶

13

$$\sqrt{1+\frac{5}{4}}-\sqrt{2-\frac{14}{25}}+\sqrt{1+\frac{36}{64}}=A$$

Based on the expression above what is the value of A?

A) $\frac{31}{20}$

B) $\frac{3}{2}$

C) 1

D) $\frac{21}{5}$

14

$$\left(2\sqrt{0{,}09}+4\sqrt[3]{0{,}027}\right)\cdot\frac{1}{9}$$

What is the result of the operation given above?

A) $\frac{1}{5}$

B) $\frac{1}{3}$

C) $\frac{9}{5}$

D) $\frac{10}{3}$

15

$$\sqrt{4}-\sqrt[3]{-8}+\sqrt{(-2)^4}\div\sqrt[4]{(-4)^2}$$

What is the result of the operation given above?

A) 2

B) 3

C) 4

D) 6

16

$$\sqrt{2+\sqrt[4]{14-\sqrt[3]{-8}}}$$

What is the result of the operation given above?

A) 0

B) 1

C) 2

D) 4

17

$$m=\sqrt{9m+7}-3$$

$+3 \qquad +3$

What is the sum of all solutions to the equation above?

$(m+3)^2=(\sqrt{9m+7})^2$

$m^2+6m+9=9m+7$

$-9m-7 \quad -9m-7$

$m^2-3m+2=0$

$(m-2)(m-1)=0$

$m=2 \quad m=1 \quad 2+1=3$

A) 1
B) 2
C) 3
D) 4

18

$$a=\sqrt{2}$$
$$b=\sqrt{7}$$
$$c=\sqrt{56}$$

What is the value of $\dfrac{c}{a^3b}$?

$\dfrac{\sqrt{56}}{(\sqrt{2})^3\sqrt{7}}=\dfrac{\sqrt{56}}{\sqrt{8}\cdot\sqrt{7}}=\dfrac{\sqrt{56}}{\sqrt{56}}=1$

A) 1
B) 2
C) 7
D) $\sqrt{2}$

19

$$m=\sqrt{12}-\sqrt{8}=2\sqrt{3}-2\sqrt{2}$$
$$n=\sqrt{27}+\sqrt{18}=3\sqrt{3}+3\sqrt{2}$$

Based on the expressions given above, what is the value of *mn*?

$2(\sqrt{3}-\sqrt{2})\cdot 3(\sqrt{3}+\sqrt{2})$

$6(3-2)=6$

A) 6
B) 12
C) 18
D) 30

20

$$\sqrt{\frac{4^7+4^7+4^7+4^7}{2^6+2^6+2^6+2^6}}=\mathrm{A}$$

$2^6=(2^2)^3=4^3$

According to the equation above what is the value of A?

$\sqrt{\dfrac{4^1\cdot 4^7}{4^1\cdot 4^3}}=\sqrt{\dfrac{4^8}{4^4}}=\sqrt{4^4}=4^2=16$

A) 2
B) 4
C) 16
D) 64

21

$$\frac{\sqrt[4]{(-3)^4}-\sqrt{(-5)^2}}{\sqrt[5]{(-0.2)^5}}$$

$\sqrt[n]{a^n}=a$ if n is odd; $\sqrt[n]{a^n}=|a|$ if n is even

What is the value of the operation given above?

$\dfrac{3^{\frac{4}{4}}-5^{\frac{2}{2}}}{\left(-\frac{1}{5}\right)^{\frac{5}{5}}}=\dfrac{3-5}{-\frac{1}{5}}=-2\cdot\dfrac{-5}{1}=10$

A) - 40
B) - 10
C) 4
D) 10

22

$$a=\sqrt{3}+1$$
$$b=\sqrt{3}-1$$

What is the equivalent of $\dfrac{a+b}{a\cdot b}$?

$\dfrac{\sqrt{3}+1+\sqrt{3}-1}{(\sqrt{3}+1)\cdot(\sqrt{3}-1)}=\dfrac{2\sqrt{3}}{3-1}=\dfrac{2\sqrt{3}}{2}=\sqrt{3}$

A) $\sqrt{3}$
B) $\dfrac{\sqrt{3}}{3}$
C) $\dfrac{1}{3}$
D) $\dfrac{1}{4}$

CONTINUE ▶

23

$$\left(\sqrt{m}\cdot\sqrt[4]{m}\right)^2$$

If $m = 4$, what is the value of the operation given above?

$\left(\sqrt{4}\cdot\sqrt[4]{4}\right)^2=\left(4^{\frac{1}{2}}\cdot 4^{\frac{1}{4}}\right)^2$

$=4^{\frac{2}{2}}\cdot 4^{\frac{2}{4}}$

$=4\cdot\left(2^2\right)^{\frac{2}{4}}$

$=4\cdot 2^{\frac{4}{4}}=4\cdot 2=8$

A) 2
B) 4
C) 8
D) 16

24

$$\sqrt[4]{(-3)^4}+\sqrt[3]{(-2)^3}+\sqrt[6]{(-4)^6}$$

even, odd, even

What is the value of the operation given above?

$\sqrt[n]{a^n}=a$ if n is odd; $\sqrt[n]{a^n}=|a|$ if n is even

$\sqrt[4]{3^4}+\sqrt[3]{-2^3}+\sqrt[6]{4^6}$

$3^{\frac{4}{4}}+(-2)^{\frac{3}{3}}+4^{\frac{6}{6}}$

$3^1+(-2)^1+4^1=3-2+4=5$

A) -7
B) -6
C) 5
D) 9

25

$$\sqrt[3]{(-8)^2}+\sqrt[3]{-3^3}+\sqrt{(-6)^2}$$

$4-3+6=7$

What is the result of the operation given above?

$\sqrt[n]{a^n}=a$ if n is odd; $\sqrt[n]{a^n}=|a|$ if n is even

A) -1
B) 6
C) 7
D) 9

26

$$(x-5)^2=\left(\sqrt{4x+1}\right)^2$$

Based on the equation above what is the value of x?

$x^2-10x+25=4x+1$

$-4x-1 \quad -4x-1$

$x^2-14x+24=0$

$(x-12)\cdot(x-2)=0$

$x=12 \quad x=2$

$2-5\neq\sqrt{4\cdot2+1}$

A) 2
B) 12
C) 2 or 12
D) None of the above

27

$$x-\sqrt{2x}=4$$

$-4+\sqrt{2x} \quad -4+\sqrt{2x}$

Based on the equation above, what is the value of x?

$(x-4)^2=\left(\sqrt{2x}\right)^2$

$x^2-8x+16=2x$

$-2x \quad -2x$

$x^2-10x+16=0$

$(x-8)\cdot(x-2)=0$

$x=8 \quad x=2$ does not work

A) 6
B) 8
C) 9
D) 12

28

If $a=\sqrt{2}+1$, what is the equivalent of $a(a-1)(a-2)$?

$\left(\sqrt{2}+1\right)\cdot\left(\sqrt{2}+1-1\right)\cdot\left(\sqrt{2}+1-2\right)$

$\left(\sqrt{2}+1\right)\cdot\left(\sqrt{2}-1\right)\cdot\left(\sqrt{2}\right)$

$(2-1)\cdot\sqrt{2}=\sqrt{2}$

A) $-\sqrt{2}$
B) 1
C) $\sqrt{2}$
D) $3+\sqrt{2}$

29

$$\frac{\sqrt{\frac{7}{9}-\frac{3}{4}}}{\sqrt{\frac{4}{9}-\frac{7}{16}}}$$

What is the result of the operation given above?

A) 0.5

B) 1

C) 2

D) 4

$$\frac{\sqrt{\frac{7\cdot4}{9\cdot4}-\frac{3\cdot9}{4\cdot9}}}{\sqrt{\frac{4\cdot16}{9\cdot16}-\frac{7\cdot9}{16\cdot9}}}=\frac{\sqrt{\frac{28-27}{36}}}{\sqrt{\frac{64-63}{144}}}=\frac{1}{6}\cdot\frac{12}{1}=2$$

30

$$a+b=\sqrt{7}$$
$$b-c=\sqrt{5}$$

What is the value of $b^2-bc+ab-ac$?

A) $\sqrt{2}$

B) $\sqrt{35}$

C) $\sqrt{7}-\sqrt{5}$

D) 2

$b(b-c)+a(b-c)$

$(b-c)\cdot(a+b)$

$\sqrt{5}\cdot\sqrt{7}=\sqrt{35}$

31

$$a=\sqrt{6}+1$$
$$b=\sqrt{6}-1$$

What is the equivalent of $\frac{a}{b}+\frac{b}{a}$?

A) 2

B) 3

C) $\frac{4}{5}$

D) $\frac{14}{5}$

$$\frac{(\sqrt{6}+1)(\sqrt{6}+1)}{(\sqrt{6}-1)(\sqrt{6}+1)}+\frac{(\sqrt{6}-1)(\sqrt{6}-1)}{(\sqrt{6}+1)(\sqrt{6}-1)}$$

$$\frac{6+2\sqrt{6}+1+6-2\sqrt{6}+1}{6-1}=\frac{14}{5}$$

32

$$\sqrt[4]{4^8+\frac{4^8-4^{10}}{2^4}}$$

$2^4=(2^2)^2=4^2$

What is the result of the operation given above?

A) 4

B) 8

C) 16

D) 32

$$\sqrt[4]{\frac{4^8\cdot4^2}{4^2}+\frac{4^8-4^{10}}{4^2}}=\sqrt[4]{\frac{4^{10}+4^8-4^{10}}{4^2}}$$

$$=\sqrt[4]{\frac{4^8}{4^2}}=\sqrt[4]{4^8\cdot4^{-2}}$$

$$=4^{\frac{6}{4}}=2^{\frac{2\cdot6}{4}}=2^3=8$$

33

$$a=\sqrt{2}+\sqrt{24}$$
$$b=\sqrt{6}+\sqrt{20}$$
$$c=\sqrt{8}+\sqrt{18}$$

$2+24=6+20=8+18$

Which of the following order is correct about $a, b,$ and c given above?

A) $b=a=c$

B) $a<b<c$

C) $b<c=a$

D) $c<a<b$

Sum of the numbers inside the square roots are equal, but sum of the square roots will not be equal. It will be maximized when numbers are closer to each other.

34

$$\sqrt[x]{a}\cdot\sqrt[y]{a}$$

What is the equivalent of the expression above?

A) $\sqrt[xy]{a}$

B) $\sqrt[xy]{a^2}$

C) $\sqrt[x+y]{a^{xy}}$

D) $\sqrt[xy]{a^{x+y}}$

$$a^{\frac{1}{x}}\cdot a^{\frac{1}{y}}=a^{\frac{1\cdot y}{x\cdot y}+\frac{1\cdot x}{y\cdot x}}$$

$$=a^{\frac{x+y}{xy}}$$

$$=\sqrt[x\cdot y]{a^{x+y}}$$

CONTINUE ▶

35

$$\sqrt{3-\sqrt{7}}\cdot\sqrt{3+\sqrt{5}}\cdot\sqrt{3+\sqrt{7}}\cdot\sqrt{3-\sqrt{5}}$$

$\sqrt{3-\sqrt{7}}\cdot\sqrt{3+\sqrt{7}}\cdot\sqrt{3+\sqrt{5}}\cdot\sqrt{3-\sqrt{5}}$

What is the result of the operation given above?

$\sqrt{(3-\sqrt{7})(3+\sqrt{7})}\cdot\sqrt{(3+\sqrt{5})(3-\sqrt{5})}$

$\sqrt{9-7}\cdot\sqrt{9-5}$

$\sqrt{2}\cdot\sqrt{4}$

$2\sqrt{2}$

A) 2
B) $2\sqrt{2}$
C) 4
D) 8

36

$x-3\geq 0$, $+3\ \ +3$, $x\geq 3$

$3-x\geq 0$, $-3\ \ -3$, $\frac{-x}{-1}\geq\frac{-3}{-1}$, $x\leq 3$

$$\frac{\sqrt{x-3}+\sqrt{3-x}+4x}{x-1}=A$$

If A is a real number, what is the value of A?

$x\geq 3$ and $x\leq 3$; so $x=3$

$\frac{\sqrt{3-3}+\sqrt{3-3}+4\cdot 3}{3-1}=\frac{12}{2}=A$

$A=6$

A) 3
B) 4
C) 6
D) 12

37

$$A=\left(\sqrt{2}-\sqrt{3}+1\right)^2\cdot\left(\sqrt{2}+\sqrt{3}+1\right)^2$$

$A=\left((1+\sqrt{2}-\sqrt{3})\cdot(1+\sqrt{2}+\sqrt{3})\right)^2$

What is the value of A ?

$A=\left((1+\sqrt{2})^2-(\sqrt{3})^2\right)^2$

$A=\left(1+2\sqrt{2}+2-3\right)^2$

$A=\left(2\sqrt{2}\right)^2=4\cdot 2=8$

A) $\sqrt{2}+1$
B) $4+4\sqrt{2}$
C) $4\sqrt{2}$
D) 8

38

$$\sqrt{2x+9}-\sqrt{17-3x}$$

$2x+9\geq 0$, $-9\ \ -9$, $\frac{2x}{2}\geq\frac{-9}{2}$, $x\geq\frac{-9}{2}$

$17-3x\geq 0$, $-17\ \ -17$, $\frac{-3x}{-3}\geq\frac{-17}{-3}$, $x\geq\frac{-17}{-3}$, $x\geq\frac{17}{3}$

For how many integer values of x is the operation above defined in real numbers?

-4.5 ... 5.66: $-4, -3, -2, -1, 0, 1, 2, 3, 4, 5$

10 integer values.

A) 10
B) 11
C) 12
D) 13

39

If $m=\sqrt{3}-1$ and $n=\sqrt{3}+1$ what is $\frac{m}{n}-\frac{n}{m}$?

$\frac{(\sqrt{3}-1)(\sqrt{3}-1)}{(\sqrt{3}+1)(\sqrt{3}-1)}-\frac{(\sqrt{3}+1)(\sqrt{3}+1)}{(\sqrt{3}-1)(\sqrt{3}+1)}$

$\frac{3-2\sqrt{3}+1-(3+2\sqrt{3}+1)}{3-1}$

$\frac{3-2\sqrt{3}+1-3-2\sqrt{3}-1}{3-1}=\frac{-4\sqrt{3}}{2}=-2\sqrt{3}$

A) $\sqrt{3}$
B) $-\sqrt{3}$
C) $-2\sqrt{3}$
D) -1

40

$$f(m)=\sqrt{m^2+16}$$

Which of the following values of x is not in the range of $f(m)$?

$m^2+16\geq 16$ so $f(m)\geq\sqrt{16}$

$f(m)$ can NOT be 3.

A) 3
B) 4
C) 5
D) 6

41

$$mn = 144$$

$$\frac{1}{\sqrt{m}} + \frac{1}{\sqrt{n}} = \frac{7}{12}$$

$\frac{\sqrt{n}+\sqrt{m}}{\sqrt{mn}} = \frac{7}{12}$

What is the value of $m + n$ in the equation given above?

$\frac{\sqrt{n}+\sqrt{m}}{\sqrt{144}} = \frac{7}{12}$ $\frac{\sqrt{n}+\sqrt{m}}{12} = \frac{7}{12}$

$(\sqrt{n}+\sqrt{m})^2 = (7)^2$ $m+n+2\sqrt{mn} = 49$

$m+n+2\sqrt{144} = 49$

$m+n+24 = 49$

$-24 \quad -24$

$m+n = 25$

A) 7
B) 9
C) 16
D) 25

42

$$\sqrt{2019 \cdot 2015 + 4}$$

What is the value of the operation given above?

$\sqrt{(2017+2)\cdot(2017-2)+4}$

$\sqrt{2017^2 - 2^2 + 4} = 2017$

A) 2013
B) 2015
C) 2017
D) 2019

43

$$a = \sqrt{2}$$
$$b = \sqrt{6}$$
$$c = \sqrt{10}$$

How to get 15;

$\frac{6 \cdot 10}{2 \cdot 2} = 15$

What is the value of $\sqrt{15}$ in terms of a, b and c?

$\frac{b \cdot c}{a \cdot a} = \frac{\sqrt{6}\cdot\sqrt{10}}{\sqrt{2}\cdot\sqrt{2}}$

$\frac{\sqrt{60}}{\sqrt{4}} = \sqrt{\frac{60}{4}} = \sqrt{15}$

A) $\frac{a^2 b}{c}$
B) $\frac{ac^2}{b}$
C) $\frac{bc}{a^2}$
D) $\frac{a+b}{c}$

44

The sum of the square root of two integers is 7. If the square root of the sum of the integers is 5, then what is the product of these integers?

$\sqrt{a}+\sqrt{b} = 7$ $\sqrt{a+b} = 5$

$(\sqrt{a}+\sqrt{b})^2 = (7)^2$ $(\sqrt{a+b})^2 = (5)^2$

$a+b+2\sqrt{ab} = 49$ $a+b = 25$

$25 + 2\sqrt{ab} = 49$, $-25 \quad -25$ $\frac{2\sqrt{ab}}{2} = \frac{24}{2}$

$\sqrt{ab} = 12$

$(\sqrt{ab})^2 = (12)^2$ $ab = 144$

A) 9
B) 16
C) 64
D) 144

CONTINUE ▶

45

$$3 \cdot \frac{\sqrt{x}}{3} = 2\sqrt{5} \cdot 3$$

What is the value of x in the equation given above?

$(\sqrt{x})^2 = (6\sqrt{5})^2$ $x = 6 \cdot 5$ $x = 180$

46

$$m = 3\sqrt{2} \qquad 4m = \sqrt{2x}$$

What is the value of x in the equation given above?

$(4 \cdot 3\sqrt{2})^2 = (\sqrt{2x})^2$ $16 \cdot 9 \cdot 2 = 2 \cdot x$

$x = 144$

47

$$\frac{\sqrt{n}}{4\sqrt{3}} = \frac{2}{1}$$

What is the value of n in the equation given above?

$(\sqrt{n})^2 = (8\sqrt{3})^2$ $n = 64 \cdot 3 = 192$

48

$$A = \frac{2}{\sqrt{3}-2} - \frac{2}{\sqrt{3}+2}$$

What is the value of A^2?

$$A = \frac{2(\sqrt{3}+2)}{(\sqrt{3}-2)(\sqrt{3}+2)} - \frac{2(\sqrt{3}-2)}{(\sqrt{3}+2)(\sqrt{3}-2)}$$

$$A = \frac{2\sqrt{3}+4-2\sqrt{3}+4}{3-4} = \frac{8}{-1} = -8$$

$A^2 = (-8)^2 = 64$

49

The sum of an integer and three times its square root is 40. What is the square root of the integer?

$40 = x + 3\sqrt{x}$
$-x \quad -x$

$(40-x)^2 = (3\sqrt{x})^2$

$1{,}600 - 80x + x^2 = 9x$
$-9x \quad -9x$

$x^2 - 89x + 1{,}600 = 0$

$(x-64)(x-25) = 0$ $x = 25$ $\sqrt{x} = \sqrt{25}$

$x = 5$

50

The square root of a positive number is the same as the number divided by 20. What is the square root of that number?

$\sqrt{x} = \frac{x}{20}$ $20 \cdot \sqrt{x} = \frac{x}{20} \cdot 20$

$(20 \cdot \sqrt{x})^2 = (x)^2$ $400x = x^2$

$400 = x$

$\sqrt{x} = \sqrt{400} = 20$

51

$$\frac{n}{6\sqrt{5}} - \frac{2\sqrt{5}}{3} = \frac{2}{\sqrt{5}}$$

What is the value of *n* in the equation given above?

$$\frac{n}{6\sqrt{5}} - \frac{2\sqrt{5}\cdot 2\sqrt{5}}{3\cdot 2\sqrt{5}} = \frac{6\cdot 2}{6\cdot \sqrt{5}}$$

$n - 20 = 12$
$+20 \quad +20$
$n = 32$

52

$$\sqrt{7-\sqrt{13}}\cdot\sqrt{7+\sqrt{13}}$$

What is the value of the radical equation given above?

$$\sqrt{(7-\sqrt{13})(7+\sqrt{13})} = \sqrt{49-13} = \sqrt{36} = 6$$

CONTINUE ▶

Math Test – Calculator

For multiple choice questions, choose the best answers from the choices after you solve the questions. Check your answers from the answer key.

For free responce questions, find your answer, write it in the space provided below and finally check it from the answer key.

NOTES

1. Calculator **is allowed**.

2. All variables are real numbers unless otherwise indicated.

3. Figures of this test are drawn to scale unless otherwise indicated.

4. Figures of this test lie in a plane.

5. Unless otherwise stated, the domain of function f is the set of all real numbers x for which $f(x)$ is a real number.

REFERENCE

$A = \pi r^2$ $\qquad$ $A = \ell w$ $\qquad$ $A = \dfrac{1}{2}bh$ $\qquad$ $c^2 = a^2 + b^2$ $\qquad$ Special Right Triangles

$C = 2\pi r$

$V = \ell wh$ $\qquad$ $V = \pi r^2 h$ $\qquad$ $V = \dfrac{4}{3}\pi r^3$ $\qquad$ $V = \dfrac{1}{3}\pi r^2 h$ $\qquad$ $V = \dfrac{1}{3}\ell wh$

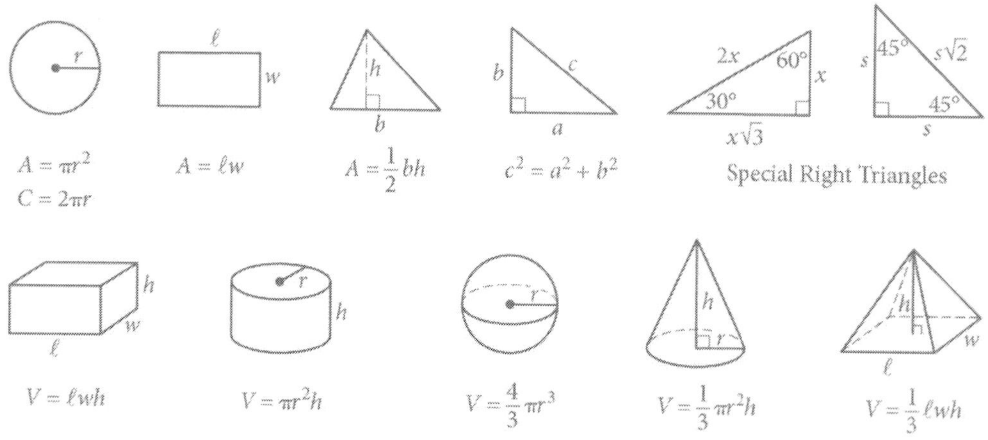

The number of degrees of a circle is 360.

The number of radians of a circle is 2π.

The sum of the angles of a triangle is 180 degrees.

CONTINUE ▶

1

If a population of P triples every year, which of the following is an expression for the size of population after n months?

A) $P(3^{\frac{n}{12}})$

B) $P(3^{\frac{12}{n}})$

C) $P(3^{n})$

D) $P(3^{12n})$

2

$$F(t) = 1{,}200\,(1.05)^{t}$$

The function defined above gives the future value, $F(t)$, of an investment after t years. What is the initial value of the investment?

A) 1.05

B) 1,200

C) 1,260

D) 1,201.5

3

The functions $y=6\left(\frac{2}{5}\right)^{x}$ and $y=\frac{1}{6}\left(\frac{4}{3}\right)^{x}$ are graphed in the xy – plane. Which of the following statements describes whether the graph of each function is always increasing or decreasing for $x>0$?

A) Both graphs are always increasing.

B) Both graphs are always decreasing.

C) The graph of $y=6\left(\frac{2}{5}\right)^{x}$ is always increasing and the graph of $y=\frac{1}{6}\left(\frac{4}{3}\right)^{x}$ is always decreasing.

D) The graph of $y=6\left(\frac{2}{5}\right)^{x}$ is always decreasing and the graph of $y=\frac{1}{6}\left(\frac{4}{3}\right)^{x}$ is always increasing.

4

$$P(t)=P_0\left(1+\frac{r}{100}\right)^{n}$$

The formula given above models the population of a city n years after an initial population of P_0 people is counted. The population grows at a constant rate of $r\%$ per year. The population of the city was 860,000 in 2010. Assume the population grows at a constant rate of 4% per year. According to this formula, which of the following is an expression for the population of the city in the year 2020?

A) $860{,}000(4)^{10}$

B) $860{,}000(1.04)^{10}$

C) $(860{,}000\times0.6)^{10}$

D) $(860{,}000\times1.04)^{10}$

CONTINUE ▶

5

An exponential function is always increasing for $x > 0$ and its y intercept is (0,4). Which of the following could be the equation of this exponential function?

A) $y = 2(0.5)^x$

B) $y = 4(0.5)^x$

C) $y = 3(2)^x + 1$

D) $y = 4(2)^x + 2$

6

In 2012, the number of cell phone subscribers in the small town of Molnar was 1,500. The number of subscribers increased by 60% per year after 2012. How many subscribers were expected in Molnar in 2015?

A) 1,800

B) 2,400

C) 3,840

D) 6,144

7

The half-life of a radioactive substance is 6 days. If you have 200mg of a substance, how many mg of it will decay after 18 days?

A) 25

B) 100

C) 150

D) 175

8

The equation $P(x) = 865(0.95)^x$ represents the value, in dollars, of a laptop after x months it is released. Megan plans to buy the laptop two months after the release date to save some money. How much more will she save, to the nearest dollars, if she waits one more month and buys it three months after it is released?

A) \$39

B) \$85

C) \$124

D) \$721

CONTINUE ▶

9

q	$N(q)$
0	1400
1	2800
2	5600
3	11200
4	22400

The relationship netween $N(q)$ and q is defined in the chart above. Which of the following equations best describes this relationship?

A) $N(q) = 1400 \times (2)^q$
B) $N(q) = 1400 \times 2q$
C) $N(q) = 1400 \times 2q^2$
D) $N(q) = 1400 \times q^2$

10

Time (weeks)	Population
0	200
5	2,000
10	20,000
15	200,000

The population of mosquitoes in a swamp in Masai Mara in Kenya is estimated throughout fifteen weeks.

Population data over fifteen weeks is given in the table above. Which of the following relationships between time and the estimated population of mosquitoes describes the population growth best during these fifteen weeks?

A) Increasing linear
B) Decreasing linear
C) Exponential growth
D) Exponential decay

11

$$n = 2^x$$

One of the most common examples of exponential growth deals with bacteria. Bacteria splits into two new cells very rapidly. The formula given above shows that one bacteria doubles every two hours. If one bacteria starts splitting inside a container, how many bacteria will be in the container by the end of one day, which is 24 hours?

A) 1,024

B) 2,048

C) 4,096

D) 8,192

12

The population of Burmese python grows 2.25% per year. If its current population in Everglades is 20 million, which function models the population, P, measured in millions, as a function of the number of years t, into the future?

A) $P(t) = 20(2.25)^t$

B) $P(t) = 20(0.225)^t$

C) $P(t) = 20(1.0225)^t$

D) $P(t) = 20(102.25)^t$

13

$$f(x) = 4\left(\frac{3}{5}\right)^x$$

An exponential function is given above. Which of the following about this function is correct?

A) It is an exponential growth function.

B) It is an exponential decay function.

C) $f(0) = \frac{12}{5}$

D) $f(2) > f(1)$

14

$$m = d(1 + r)^n$$

A bank account balance, *m*, for an account starting with *d* dollars, earning an annual interest rate, *r*, and left untouched for *n* years can be calculated with the exponential growth formula given above.

If the account starts at $200 and has an annual rate of 5%, what will be the money left in the account for 6 years?

A) 231.50

B) 243.10

C) 255.25

D) 268.02

15

$$B = 70(M)^{\frac{3}{4}}$$

The formula given above, relates the basal metabolic rate, B, measured in kilocalories per day, of an animal to its body mass, M, measured in kilograms. If the body mass of a crocodile is 10^4 times that of an hamster, which of the following best compares their basal metabolic rates?

A) The basal metabolic rate of the crocodile is 0.75 times that of the hamster.
B) The basal metabolic rate of the crocodile is 3 times that of the hamster.
C) The basal metabolic rate of the crocodile is $10^{0.75}$ times that of the hamster.
D) The basal metabolic rate of the crocodile is 10^3 times that of the hamster.

16

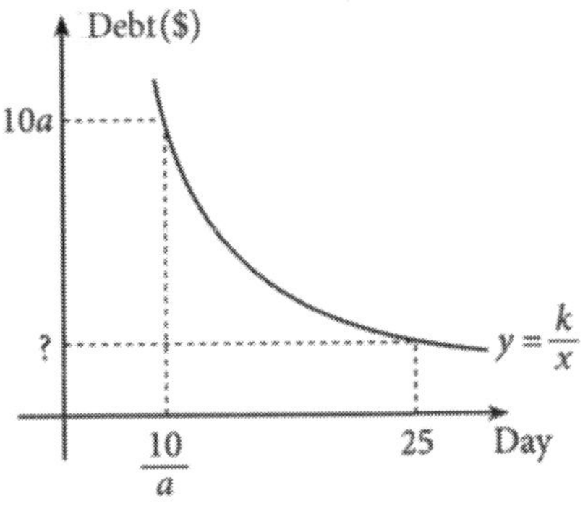

The graph above shows the debt of a company for the day. What is the debt of the company on day 25?

A) 2
B) 4
C) 8
D) 10

17

A sociologist estimates that, starting from the present, the population of the county will decrease by 20 percent every 10 years. If the present population of the county is 150,000, which of the following expressions represents the sociologist's estimate of the population of the county t years after from now?

A) $150{,}000(0.2)^{10t}$
B) $150{,}000(0.8)^{\frac{t}{10}}$
C) $150{,}000(1.2)^{\frac{t}{10}}$
D) $150{,}000(0.9)^{10t}$

18

$$P(t) = 3.6 \cdot 2^{0.05t}$$

The price, $P(t)$, for a particular product t years after 2010 is modeled by the function given above. Based on this function, after 2010, how many years will it take for the price to quadruple?

A) 4
B) 10
C) 20
D) 40

19

$$s(t) = 30(2)^{0.5t}$$

The number of seedlings in a greenhouse is observed, and its population growth, s, t hours from the first observation, is modeled by the function given above.

How much does the seedling population increase from $t = 2$ to $t = 6$?

A) 60
B) 120
C) 180
D) 240

20

Bacteria can multiply very quickly. A certain type of bacteria has a doubling time of 15 minutes. If 100 bacteria are left in a container, how many bacteria will grow between 30 and 60 minutes?

A) 400
B) 800
C) 1,200
D) 1,600

21

t	0	1	2	3
$F(t)$	128	16	2	0.25

The table above shows some values for the function F. If $F(t) = m \cdot 2^{-nt}$ for positive constants m and n, what is the value of $m + n$?

A) 3
B) 125
C) 128
D) 131

22

$$t^2 = C \cdot r^3$$

The equation given above represents Kepler's 3rd law of planetary motion. The equation relates the time, t, in days, that a planet takes to revolve once around the sun to the distance, r, in kilometers, of that planet from the sun.

Jupiter is approximately 4 times as distant from the sun as Venus. How many times longer would Jupiter's revolution time be than the revolution time of Venus?

A) 2
B) 4
C) 8
D) 16

23

$$n(p)=\frac{8400}{4p+c}$$

The function above gives the sales volume of a digital watch, where n is the number of digital watches sold, p is the price per digital watch in dollars, and c is a constant.

According to the projections, if 42,000 digital watches are sold at $15 per digital watch, how many digital watches will be sold at $16 per digital watch?

A) 2,000
B) 3,000
C) 4,000
D) 6,000

24

A radioactive isotope has a half-life of 2 years. If there is a sample of 400g in 2018, how many years later will there remain only 50g?

25

A cell phone company invests $200,000 in equipment to produce a new line of smartphones. Each phone costs $120 to produce and is sold for $620.

How many phones must be sold before the business breaks even?

26

The number of mobile device users worldwide has grown to five billion, with the latest billion users being added in just the last four years, according to new statistics released by GSMA in 2018.

If mobile users continue to increase by 4% yearly, how many billion users will be expected in 2021?

27

The population of a bacteria culture doubles every 45 minutes. How long will it take for the population to grow from 200 to 12,800 bacteria?

28

Angelina plans to surround a rectangular area of 72 square feet using 36 ft fencing. What is the length of the rectangular area?

SECTION 4 - NONLINEAR GRAPHS & EXPRESSIONS

#	Answer	Topic	Subtopic
1	A	TB	S2
2	B	TB	S2
3	D	TB	S2
4	B	TB	S2
5	C	TB	S2
6	D	TB	S2
7	D	TB	S2

#	Answer	Topic	Subtopic
8	A	TB	S2
9	A	TB	S2
10	C	TB	S2
11	C	TB	S2
12	C	TB	S2
13	B	TB	S2
14	D	TB	S2

#	Answer	Topic	Subtopic
15	D	TB	S2
16	B	TB	S2
17	B	TB	S2
18	D	TB	S2
19	C	TB	S2
20	C	TB	S2
21	D	TB	S2

#	Answer	Topic	Subtopic
22	C	TB	S2
23	A	TB	S2
24	6	TB	S2
25	400	TB	S2
26	5.62	TB	S2
27	4.5	TB	S2
28	12	TB	S2

Topics & Subtopics

Code	Description
SB2	Nonlinear Graphs & Expressions

Code	Description
TB	Passport to Advanced Mathematics

1

If a population of P triples every year, which of the following is an expression for the size of population after n months?

n months is $\frac{n}{12}$ years

Growth factor is 3.

A) $P(3^{\frac{n}{12}})$

B) $P(3^{\frac{12}{n}})$

C) $P(3^n)$

D) $P(3^{12n})$

$P=(3)^{\frac{n}{12}}$

2

$$F(t) = 1{,}200(1.05)^t$$

F(0); initial value is 1,200

The function defined above gives the future value, $F(t)$, of an investment after t years. What is the initial value of the investment?

A) 1.05

B) 1,200

C) 1,260

D) 1,201.5

3

The functions $y=6\left(\frac{2}{5}\right)^x$ and $y=\frac{1}{6}\cdot\left(\frac{4}{3}\right)^x$ are graphed in the xy-plane. Which of the following statements describes whether the graph of each function is always increasing or decreasing for $x>0$?

A) Both graphs are always increasing.

B) Both graphs are always decreasing.

C) The graph of $y=6\left(\frac{2}{5}\right)^x$ is always increasing and the graph of $y=\frac{1}{6}\cdot\left(\frac{4}{3}\right)^x$ is always decreasing.

D) The graph of $y=6\left(\frac{2}{5}\right)^x$ is always decreasing and the graph of $y=\frac{1}{6}\cdot\left(\frac{4}{3}\right)^x$ is always increasing.

Growth factor; $\frac{2}{5}<1 \to$ decreasing

Growth factor; $\frac{4}{3}>1 \to$ increasing

4

$$P(t)=P_0\left(1+\frac{r}{100}\right)^n$$

The formula given above models the population of a city n years after an initial population of P_0 people is counted. The population grows at a constant rate of r% per year. The population of the city was 860,000 in 2010. Assume the population grows at a constant rate of 4% per year. According to this formula, which of the following is an expression for the population of the city in the year 2020?

$n=2020-2010=10$ $r=4$ $P_0=860{,}000$

A) $860{,}000(4)^{10}$

B) $860{,}000(1.04)^{10}$ $P(t)=860{,}000\left(1+\frac{4}{100}\right)^{10}$

C) $(860{,}000\times 0.6)^{10}$

D) $(860{,}000\times 1.04)^{10}$

5

An exponential function is always increasing for $x > 0$ and its y intercept is $(0,4)$. Which of the following could be the equation of this exponential function?

$f(x) = a^x$ increases if $a > 1$

A) $y = 2(0.5)^x$ $y(0) = 2 \cdot (0.5)^0 = 2 \cdot 1 = 2$ ☹

B) $y = 4(0.5)^x$ $0.5 < 1$ ☹

C) $y = 3(2)^x + 1$ $2 > 1$ ☺

D) $y = 4(2)^x + 2$ $y(0) = 4 \cdot 2^0 + 2 = 4 \cdot 1 + 2 = 6$ ☹

6

In 2012, the number of cell phone subscribers in the small town of Molnar was 1,500. The number of subscribers increased by 60% per year after 2012. How many subscribers were expected in Molnar in 2015?

A) 1,800 $t = 2015 - 2012 = 3$

B) 2,400 $1,500 \times (1.6)^3$

C) 3,840

D) 6,144 $6,144$

7

The half-life of a radioactive substance is 6 days. If you have 200mg of a substance, how many mg of it will decay after 18 days?

A) 25 $200 \nearrow 100 \nearrow 50 \nearrow 25$ remains

B) 100   6 days 6 days 6 days

C) 150

D) 175 $200 - 25 = 175$ decays

8

The equation $P(x) = 865(0.95)^x$ represents the value, in dollars, of a laptop after x months it is released. Megan plans to buy the laptop two months after the release date to save some money. How much more will she save, to the nearest dollars, if she waits one more month and buys it three months after it is released?

A) $39 $865 \cdot (0.95)^2 - 865 \cdot (0.95)^3$

B) $85 $780.66 - 741.63$

C) $124 $39

D) $721

9

q	$N(q)$
0	1400
1	2800
2	5600
3	11200
4	22400

No = 1,400 ×2 ×2 Growth ×2 factor is 2. ×2

It is a doubling function.

The relationship netween $N(q)$ and q is defined in the chart above. Which of the following equations best describes this relationship? $N(q) = N_0 \cdot 2^q$

$N(q) = 1{,}400 \cdot 2^q$

A) $N(q) = 1400 \times (2)^q$

B) $N(q) = 1400 \times 2q$

C) $N(q) = 1400 \times 2q^2$

D) $N(q) = 1400 \times q^2$

10

Time (weeks)	Population
0	200
5	2,000
10	20,000
15	200,000

+1,800 +18,000 +180,000

The population is increasing.

The population of mosquitoes in a swamp in Masai Mara in Kenya is estimated throughout fifteen weeks.

Population data over fifteen weeks is given in the table above. Which of the following relationships between time and the estimated population of mosquitoes describes the population growth best during these fifteen weeks? Weekly increases are not same, so it is not linear. Data shows greater increases with passing time. So it is exponential.

A) **Increasing ~~linear~~**

B) **~~Decreasing linear~~**

C) **Exponential growth**

D) **Exponential ~~decay~~**

11

$$n = 2^x$$

One of the most common examples of exponential growth deals with bacteria. Bacteria splits into two new cells very rapidly. The formula given above shows that one bacteria doubles every two hours. If one bacteria starts splitting inside a container, how many bacteria will be in the container by the end of one day which is 24 hours?

A) 1,024 $n = 2^{\frac{24}{2}} = 2^{12} = 4{,}096$
B) 2,048
C) 4,096
D) 8,192

12

The population of Burmese python grows 2.25% per year. If its current population in Everglades is 20 million, which function models the population, P, measured in millions, as a function of the number of year t, into the future? $P = P_0\left(1+\frac{r}{100}\right)^t$ $r=2.25$

A) $P(t) = 20(2.25)^t$ $1+\frac{r}{100} = 1+\frac{2.25}{100} = 1.0225$
B) $P(t) = 20(0.225)^t$
C) $P(t) = 20(1.0225)^t$ $P = 20(1.0225)^t$
D) $P(t) = 20(102.25)^t$

13

$$f(x) = 4\left(\frac{3}{5}\right)^x$$

An exponential function is given above. Which of the following about this function is correct? Growth factor; $\frac{3}{5} < 1$; decay

A) It is an exponential ~~growth~~ function.
B) It is an exponential decay function.
C) $f(0) = \frac{12}{5}$ $4\left(\frac{3}{5}\right)^0 = 4$ not $\frac{12}{5}$
D) $f(2) > f(1)$ Because it decays; $f(2) < f(1)$

14

$$m = d(1+r)^n$$

A bank account balance, *m*, for an account starting with *d* dollars, earning an annual interest rate, *r*, and left untouched for *n* years can be calculated with the exponential growth formula given above.

If the account starts at \$200 (d) and has an annual rate of 5%, what will be the money left in the account for 6 years? (t)

A) 231.50 $m = 200(1+0.05)^6$
B) 243.10 $m = 200(1.05)^6$
C) 255.25 $m = \$268.02$
D) 268.02

15

$$B = 70(M)^{\frac{3}{4}}$$

$70(M \cdot 10^4)^{\frac{3}{4}} = (10^4)^{\frac{3}{4}} \cdot 70(M \cdot 10^4) = 10^3 \cdot B$

The formula given above, relates the basal metabolic rate, B, measured in kilocalories per day, of an animal to its body mass, M, measured in kilograms. If the body mass of a crocodile is 10^4 times that of an hamster, which of the following best compares their basal metabolic rates?

A) The basal metabolic rate of the crocodile is 0.75 times that of the hamster.
B) The basal metabolic rate of the crocodile is 3 times that of the hamster.
C) The basal metabolic rate of the crocodile is $10^{0.75}$ times that of the hamster.
D) The basal metabolic rate of the crocodile is 10^3 times that of the hamster.

16

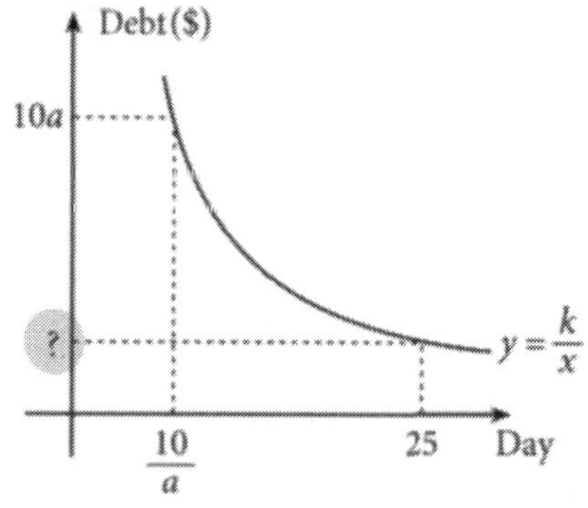

The graph above shows the debt of a company for the day. What is the debt of the company on day 25?

A) 2
B) 4
C) 8
D) 10

$\frac{10a}{1} = \frac{k}{\frac{10}{a}}$ $k = 10a \cdot \frac{10}{a}$ $k = 100$

$? = \frac{100}{25}$ $? = 4$

17

A sociologist estimates that, starting from the present, the population of the county will decrease by 20 percent every 10 years. If the present population of the county is 150,000, which of the following expressions represents the sociologist's estimate of the population of the county t years after from now?

After decrease by 20%, 80% remains.

A) $150{,}000(0.2)^{10t}$
B) $150{,}000(0.8)^{\frac{t}{10}}$
C) $150{,}000(1.2)^{\frac{t}{10}}$
D) $150{,}000(0.9)^{10t}$

# of 10 years $= \frac{t}{10}$

18

$$P(t) = 3.6 \cdot 2^{0.05t}$$

The price, $P(t)$, for a particular product t years after 2010 is modeled by the function given above. Based on this function, after 2010, how many years will it take for the price to quadruple?

4 times bigger ; $2^{0.05t} = 2^2$

A) 4
B) 10
C) 20
D) 40

$\frac{0.05t}{0.05} = \frac{2}{0.05}$ $t = 40$

19

$$s(t) = 30(2)^{0.5t}$$

The number of seedlings in a greenhouse is observed, and its population growth, s, t hours from the first observation, is modeled by the function given above.

How much does the seedling population increase from $t = 2$ to $t = 6$?

A) 60
B) 120
C) 180
D) 240

20

Bacteria can multiply very quickly. A certain type of bacteria has a doubling time of 15 minutes. If 100 bacteria are left in a container, how many bacteria will grow between 30 and 60 minutes?

A) 400
B) 800
C) 1,200
D) 1,600

21

t	0	1	2	3
$F(t)$	128	16	2	0.25

The table above shows some values for the function F. If $F(t) = m \cdot 2^{-nt}$ for positive constants m and n, what is the value of $m + n$?

A) 3
B) 125
C) 128
D) 131

22

$$t^2 = C \cdot r^3$$

The equation given above represents Kepler's 3rd law of planetary motion. The equation relates the time, t, in days, that a planet takes to revolve once around the sun to the distance, r, in kilometers, of that planet from the sun.

Jupiter is approximately 4 times as distant from the sun as Venus. How many times longer would Jupiter's revolution time be than the revolution time of Venus?

A) 2
B) 4
C) 8
D) 16

CONTINUE ▶

23

$$n(p) = \frac{8400}{4p + c}$$

The function above gives the sales volume of a digital watch, where n is the number of digital watches sold, p is the price per digital watch in dollars, and c is a constant.

According to the projections, if 42,000 digital watches are sold at \$15 per digital watch, how many digital watches will be sold at \$16 per digital watch?

$42{,}000 = \frac{8{,}400}{4 \cdot 15 + c}$ $\frac{42{,}000 \cdot (60+c)}{42{,}000} = \frac{8{,}400}{42{,}000}$

$60 + c = 0.2$
$-60 \quad -60$
$c = -59.8$

A) 2,000

B) 3,000

C) 4,000

D) 6,000

$n = \frac{8{,}400}{4 \cdot 16 - 59.8} = \frac{8{,}400}{64 - 59.8} = \frac{8{,}400}{4.2} = 2{,}000$

24

A radioactive isotope has a half-life of 2 years. If there is a sample of 400g in 2018, how many years later will there remain only 50g?

2018 2020 2022 2024
400 → 200 → 100 → 50
2 years + 2 years + 2 years
6 years

25

A cell phone company invests \$200,000 in equipment to produce a new line of smartphones. Each phone costs \$120 to produce and is sold for \$620.

$200{,}000 = n \cdot (620 - 120)$

How many phones must be sold before the business breaks even?

$\frac{200{,}000}{500} = \frac{n \cdot 500}{500}$ $n = 400$

26

The number of mobile device users worldwide has grown to five billion, with the latest billion users being added in just the last four years, according to new statistics released by GSMA in 2018. $2021 - 2018 = 3$

$5 \cdot \left(1 + \frac{4}{100}\right)^3 = 5 \cdot (1.04)^3 = 5.62$

If mobile users continue to increase by 4% yearly, how many billion users will be expected in 2021?

27

The population of a bacteria culture doubles every 45 minutes. How long will it take for the population to grow from 200 to 12,800 bacteria?

$P(x) = P(0) \cdot 2^x$

$\frac{12{,}800}{200} = \frac{200}{200} \cdot 2^x$

$64 = 2^x$ $2^6 = 2^x$

$x = 6$

It doubles 6 times.

$6 \times 45\,\text{min} \times \frac{1\text{h}}{60\,\text{min}}$

4,5h

28

Angelina plans to surround a rectangular area of 72 square feet using 36 ft fencing. What is the length of the rectangular area?

$A = l \cdot w$

$72 = l \cdot (18 - l)$

w, l

$\frac{2}{2}(l + w) = \frac{36}{2}$

$l + w = 18$

$-l \quad -l$

$w = 18 - l$

$72 = 18l - l^2$

$-18l + l^2 \quad -18l + l^2$

$l^2 - 18l + 72 = 0$

$(l - 6)(l - 12) = 0$

$l = 6$ $l = 12$

CONTINUE ▶

Math Test – Calculator

DIRECTIONS

For multiple choice questions, choose the best answers from the choices after you solve the questions. Check your answers from the answer key.

For free responce questions, find your answer, write it in the space provided below and finally check it from the answer key.

NOTES

1. Calculator **is allowed**.
2. All variables are real numbers unless otherwise indicated.
3. Figures of this test are drawn to scale unless otherwise indicated.
4. Figures of this test lie in a plane.
5. Unless otherwise stated, the domain of function *f* is the set of all real numbers *x* for which *f*(*x*) is a real number.

REFERENCE

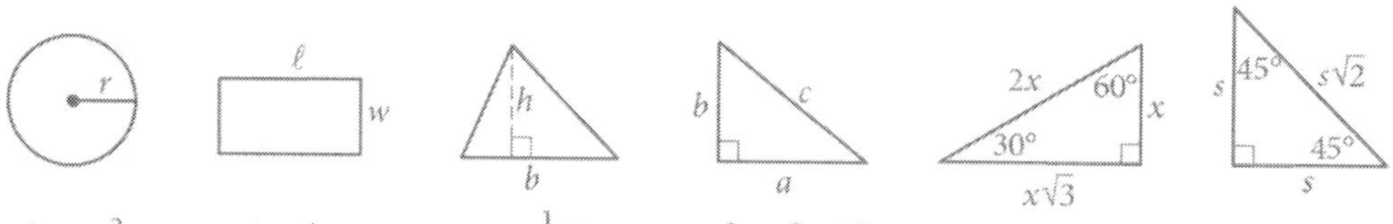

$A = \pi r^2$, $C = 2\pi r$ $A = \ell w$ $A = \frac{1}{2}bh$ $c^2 = a^2 + b^2$ Special Right Triangles

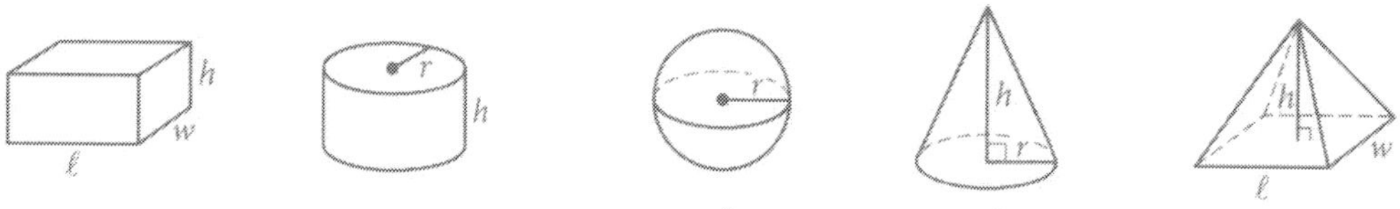

$V = \ell wh$ $V = \pi r^2 h$ $V = \frac{4}{3}\pi r^3$ $V = \frac{1}{3}\pi r^2 h$ $V = \frac{1}{3}\ell wh$

The number of degrees of a circle is 360.

The number of radians of a circle is 2π.

The sum of the angles of a triangle is 180 degrees.

1

$$K(x)= x^2 - 4x - 5$$

When $K(x)$ is shifted 2 units right and reflected over the y-axis, you get $M(x)$.

If the area bounded by the parabola $K(x)$ and the x-axis is A, then what is the area bounded by $M(x)$ and the x-axis in terms of A?

A) A
B) 2A
C) 2 + A
D) 2 - A

2

$$y = -(x+3)^2 - 2$$

The graph of the equation given above in the xy-plane is a parabola. Which of the following is true about this parabola?

A) Its minimum occurs at (3,2)
B) Its minimum occurs at (-3,2)
C) Its maximum occurs at (-3,-2)
D) Its maximum occurs at (3,-2)

3

If the vertex of a parabola is located in Quadrant I and no point in the parabola is located in Quadrant IV, which of the following must be true?

A) The x-intercept of the parabola is negative.
B) The y-intercept of the parabola is negative.
C) The coefficient for the x-squared term is positive.
D) No point in the parabola is located in Quadrant III.

4

$$y = x^2 + 6x + m$$

If the vertex of the parabola given above is 5 units away from the origin, what is the value of m?

A) -31
B) -4
C) 4
D) 5

5

$$(x + 4)^2 = 36$$

Which of the following are solutions to the quadratic equation given above?

A) -6 and 6
B) -5 and 4
C) -5 and 5
D) -10 and 2

6

$$y = 4(x + 5)(x - 7)$$

The vertex of the quadratic equation given above is (h, k). Which of the following is the value of k?

A) -36
B) 36
C) 144
D) -144

7

If $(x + k)^2 = x^2 + 23x + k^2$, what is the value of k^2?

A) 72.25
B) 90.25
C) 132.25
D) 264.50

8

$$y = 2x^2 - 4x + m - 1$$

If the minimum value of the parabola given above is 1, then what is the value of m?

A) 1
B) 2
C) 3
D) 4

9

$$v = -4t^2 - 28t + 120$$

A ball is thrown vertically upwards. The velocity of the ball is calculated by the equation given above, as a function of time, where v represents velocity, in meter per second and t represents time, in seconds.

How many seconds after throwing the ball the velocity of the ball become zero?

A) 2
B) 3
C) 4
D) 5

10

You are asked to construct a rectangular area with a 500m roll of fencing. What are the dimensions of the largest area?

A) Length is 150m, width is 100m.
B) Length is 200m, width is 50m.
C) Length and width is 125m.
D) Length and width is 150m.

11

$$2x^2 + 12x + c = 0$$

$$5x^2 + bx + 20 = 0$$

If the roots of the quadratic equations given above are the same, what is the value of $c + b$?

A) 8
B) 20
C) 30
D) 38

12

$$y = x^2 - mx + 5$$

If the symmetry axis of the parabola given above is $x = 2$, then what is the value of m?

A) -2
B) -1
C) 2
D) 4

13

$$B = 2x + 10 \qquad S = x^2 - 4x + 80$$

Buying price, B, and selling price, S, of a product, in dollars, are given above. What is the minimum profit, in dollars, that can be made by selling this item?

A) 61
B) 69
C) 81
D) 97

14

$$3(5x^2 + 1) - 4 = 7x^2 + 3$$

When solving the equation given above, Jenna wrote $3(5x^2 + 1) = 7x^2 + 7$ as her first step. Which property justifies Jenna's first step?

A) Addition property of equality
B) Commutative property of addition
C) Multiplication property of equality
D) Distributive property of multiplication over addition

15

$$h(t) = -12t^2 + 248t$$

Willian throws a ball up in a competition in a summer camp sports activity. The above quadratic equation gives the ball's height in meters, h, as a function of time, t, in seconds.

How many meters is the height of the ball 5 seconds after it has been thrown up?

A) 52
B) 300
C) 940
D) 1,240

16

$$x - 5 = \sqrt{4x + 1}$$

What value of x is a solution for the equation given above?

A) 2
B) 12
C) 2 and 12
D) None of the above

17

$$y = x^2 + (a - 3)x + 5$$

If the vertex of the parabola given above is on the line of $x = -4$, what is the value of a?

A) -5
B) -1
C) 7
D) 11

18

If $(x + 2)^2 = 11$, what is the value of $x^2 + 4x$?

A) 4
B) 7
C) 9
D) 15

19

$$y = (m - 3)x^2 - mx + 11$$

If the vertex of the parabola is on (2,7), what is the value of m?

A) 2
B) 3
C) 4
D) 6

20

$$y = (m^2 - 16)x^2 - (2m - 6)x + 12$$

If the vertex of the parabola is on the y-axis, then what is the value of m?

A) 3
B) 4
C) 6
D) 16

21

$$y = mx^2 + (m - 1)x + 3$$

If the vertex of the parabola is on the y-axis, then what is the value of m?

A) -1

B) 0

C) 1

D) 3

22

$$x^2 - bx + c = 0$$

One of the roots of the quadratic equation given above is -2. If the sum of the roots is 5, then what is the value of c?

A) -14

B) -12

C) -10

D) 7

23

$$x^2 + 3x - 4 = 0$$

Roots of the quadratic equation given above are m and n. Which of the following is the quadratic equation that has roots $m+2$ and $n+2$?

A) $x^2 + 5x - 2$

B) $x^2 - x - 6$

C) $x^2 + 7x + 6$

D) $x^2 + 7x$

24

$$y = (m-3)x^2 - 4x + 1$$

If the parabola above is tangent to the x-axis, then what is the value of m?

A) 3

B) 4

C) 6

D) 7

CONTINUE ▶

25

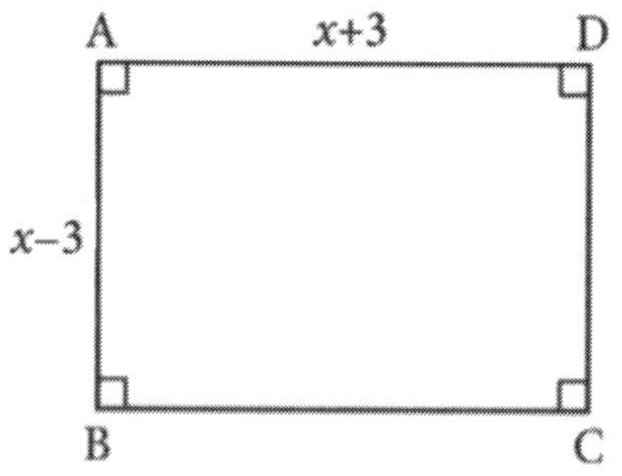

If the area of the rectangle ABCD is 36, then what is the difference in length and width?

A) 5
B) 6
C) 9
D) 16

26

$$x^2 - 5(x+3) = 0$$

Which of the following expressions best describe the quadratic equation above?

A) No solution
B) One real solution
C) Two imaginary solutions
D) Two real solutions

27

x	1	2	3	4	5	6	7
$f(x)$	7	0	-5	-8	-9	-8	-5

A quadratic function of $f(x)$ is given above. What is the sum of the roots of this function?

A) 2
B) 5
C) 8
D) 10

28

$$y = x^2 + 2$$
$$y = -x^2 + 4$$

If the graphs of the parabolas given above intersect at two different points, (m,n) and (p,q), what is the value of $m + n + p + q$?

A) 0
B) 6
C) 7
D) 8

29

$$y = -4x^2 + 16x$$

How many solutions does the quadratic equation given above have?

A) There is no solution.
B) There are two solutions.
C) There is only one solution.
D) It can not be determined.

30

$$3x^2 + y^2 = 76$$

Based on the equation given above, which of the following is a possible value for y if both x and y are integers?

A) -5
B) -1
C) 0
D) 5

31

$$y = x^2 + 6x - 16$$

Which of the following about the parabola given above is not correct?

A) It has a minimum at (-3,-25).
B) Distance between the roots is 10.
C) Average of the roots is -3.
D) Sum of the roots is -6, and multiplication of the roots is 16.

32

If $x^2 + 2xy + y^2 = 81$ and $y - 3x = -39$, which of the following could be the value of x?

A) 6
B) 8
C) 10
D) 12

33

In which of the following quadratic equations sum of the roots is equal to the product of the roots?

A) $x^2 + 3x + 2$
B) $x^2 - 3x + 3$
C) $x^2 + 4x - 5$
D) $x^2 - 4$

34

$$2x^2 - 5x = 3$$

What value of x satisfies the equation given above?

A) -1
B) 1
C) 3
D) 4

CONTINUE ▶

35

$$x^2 - mx + m + 3 = 0$$

If the quadratic equation above has a double root, what is the sum of the values of m?

A) -4
B) -2
C) 4
D) 6

36

Which of the following is the equation of the quadratic function whose roots are $1+\sqrt{6}$ and $1-\sqrt{6}$.

A) $x^2 - 2x + 5$
B) $x^2 + 2x - 5$
C) $x^2 - 2x - 5$
D) $x^2 - x - 5$

37

$$a = d^2 - 5d - 14$$

The amount of water in a pool is calculated by the equation given above as a function of day, where a represents the amount of water, in tons and d represents time, in days.

How many days will it take for the amount of water in the pool to become zero?

A) 2
B) 3
C) 5
D) 7

38

Compared to the graph of $y = x^2$, the graph of $y = (x - 3)^2 - 2$ is;

A) Shifted 3 units right and 2 units up
B) Shifted 3 units left and 2 units down
C) Shifted 3 units right and 2 units down
D) Shifted 2 units down and 3 units down

39

Which of the following expression is true for the function $y = -4\,(x - 2)^2$?

A) The y-intercept is 16.
B) The range is all negative numbers.
C) The domain is all positive numbers.
D) The graph of the function never goes below the x-axis.

40

$$l = (x + 6) \qquad w = (4 - x)$$

The length and width of a rectangle are given above. What is the maximum value for the area of this rectangle?

A) 20
B) 24
C) 25
D) 30

41

In the event of a 6-day sale of the Pi Bakery, the number of cupcakes is modeled by the quadratic function $c(x) = -0.75x^2 + 1,323$, where x is the number of working hours from 8 am to 5 pm.

Based on this information, and assuming no intervention to change the path of the number of cupcakes, which of the following statements must be true?

A) At the begining of the event there are 1,764 cupcakes.
B) The number of cupcakes is decreasing at a constant rate.
C) There will be no cupcakes left at 2 pm on Day 5 of the event.
D) The number of cupcakes will increase or decrease from the initial number after 8 am on the first day of the event.

42

Which of the following expression is NOT true for the function $h(x)=3(x-4)^2$?

A) The domain is all real numbers.
B) The range is all positive numbers.
C) The graph of the function never goes below the x-axis.
D) The graph of the function touches the x-axis where $x=-4$.

43

$$y = (x - 4)^2$$

In the xy-plane, the parabola given above intersects the line with the equation $y = 49$ at two points, A and B. What is the length of AB?

A) 3
B) 9
C) 11
D) 14

44

$$16x^2 + ax + 9$$

What value of a makes the equation given above a perfect square?

A) 3
B) 4
C) 12
D) 24

CONTINUE ▶

45

$$\frac{2x^2-3}{5-x^2}=-7$$

Which of the following statements about the equation above is true?

A) The equation has no solutions.
B) The equation has exactly one solution.
C) The equation has exactly two solutions.
D) The equation has infinitely many solutions.

46

$$P(x) = ax^2 + bx + c$$

Given the quadratic equation above, what is the value of $a + c$, if $P(1) = 10$ and $P(-1) = 6$?

A) 6
B) 8
C) 10
D) 16

47

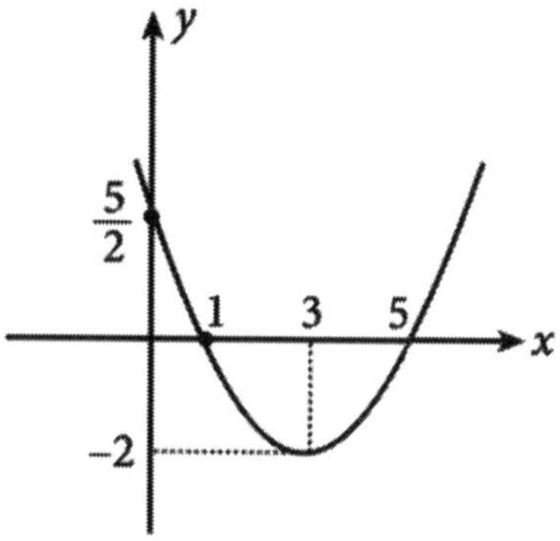

Which of the following represents the parabola shown above?

A) $f(x)=\frac{1}{2}(x-3)^2-2$
B) $f(x)=\frac{1}{2}(x+3)^2+\frac{5}{2}$
C) $f(x)=(x-3)^2+\frac{5}{2}$
D) $f(x)=(x+2)^2+3$

48

$$x^2+2x+2=0$$

Which of the following is a solution to the quadratic equation given above?

A) 1 - 2i
B) 1 + 2i
C) -1 - i
D) - i

49

$$y = mx^2 + (m - 1)x + 2m - 1$$

If the parabola given above passes through the point (2,9), what is the value of m?

A) 0.66
B) 0.75
C) 1.33
D) 1.50

50

$$x^2 + ax + b = 0$$

In the quadratic equation above $b < 0 < a$. Which of the following about the roots of this quadratic equation is true?

A) It does not have real roots.
B) The roots are equal.
C) It has two positive roots.
D) The sum of the roots is negative.

51

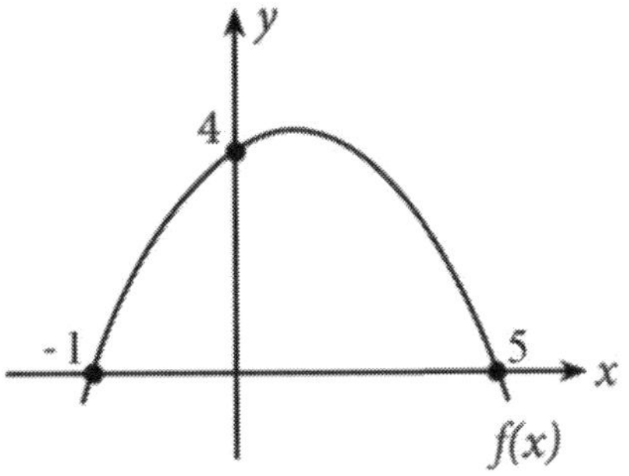

The parabola of $f(x) = ax^2 + bx + c$ is given above. What is the value of a?

A) -0.40
B) -0.80
C) -1.25
D) 4

52

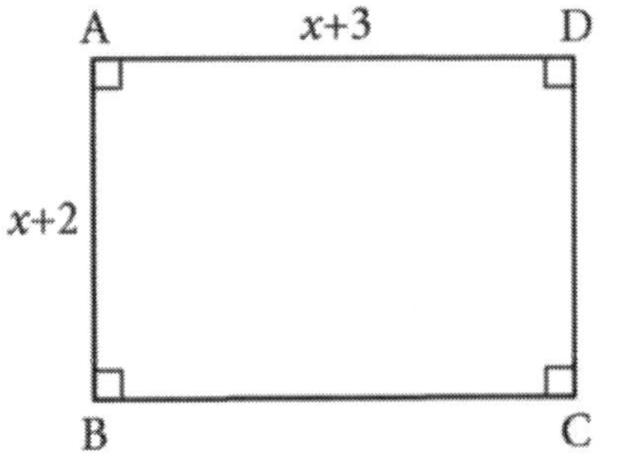

Area of the rectangle above is 100. What is the area of a square whose side is $2x + 5$?

A) 119
B) 400
C) 401
D) 449

53

$$x^2 + 13x + 36 = (x + a)(x + b)$$

In the quadratic equation given above, b is an integer. Which of the following is a possible value of b?

A) 3
B) 5
C) 7
D) 9

54

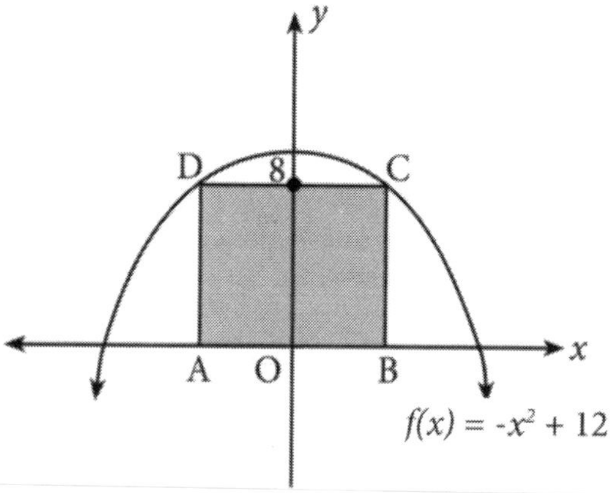

The parabola, whose formula is given above, intersects with two corners of the rectangle ABCD. What is the area of the rectangle ABCD?

A) 8
B) 16
C) 32
D) 48

55

If the points (-1,3), (0,2) and (2,12) are on the parabola $y = ax^2 + bx + c$, what is the value of $a + b + c$?

A) 1
B) 2
C) 3
D) 5

56

$$f(x) = A(x - 8)(x + 2)$$

In the quadratic function given above, A is a non-zero constant. The graph of the function in the xy plane has a vertex at the point (h,k). Which of the following is the value of k?

A) -25A
B) -16A
C) 11A
D) 64A

57

K : $-3x^2+x+4$ M : $3x^2-x+4$

L : $-3x^2+x-4$ N : $3x^2-x-4$

Which one is the equation of the parabola that passes through the points A(-1,0), B(0,4), and C(1,2)?

A) K

B) L

C) M

D) N

58

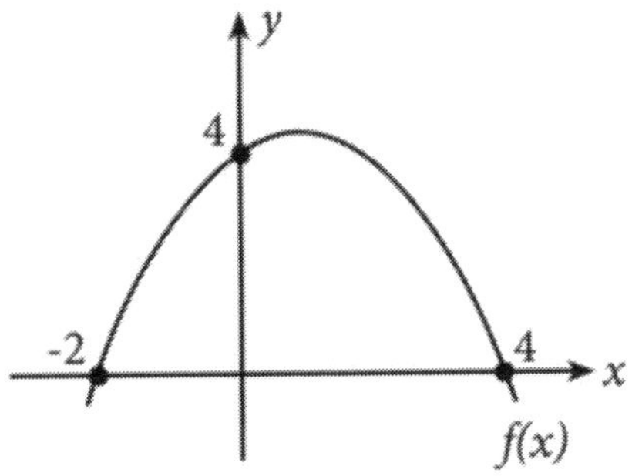

The parabola of $f(x)$ is given above. What is the maximum value of $f(x)$?

A) 4.5

B) 5

C) 5.5

D) 6

59

$$y=x^2-(m+3)x+m+2$$

If the point (-1,4) is on the parabola given above, what is the distance between the origin (0,0) and the vertex of this parabola?

A) 0

B) 1

C) 1.4

D) 2.4

60

$$y=x^2+mx+n$$

If the vertex of the parabola given above is at point (1,2), then what is the value of $m+n$?

A) -1

B) 0

C) 1

D) 3

61

If the vertex of the parabola $y = ax^2 + bx + 5$ is (1,3) then what is the value of $a + b$?

A) -2

B) 3

C) 5

D) 8

62

$$x^2 + (m-1)x + 1 = 0$$

The roots of the quadratic equation given above are a and b. If $ab + a + b = -10$, then what is the value of m?

A) -12

B) -10

C) 3

D) 12

63

$$9^x - 10 \cdot 3^x + 9 = 0$$

What is the sum of the roots of the equation given above?

A) 0

B) 1

C) 2

D) 3

64

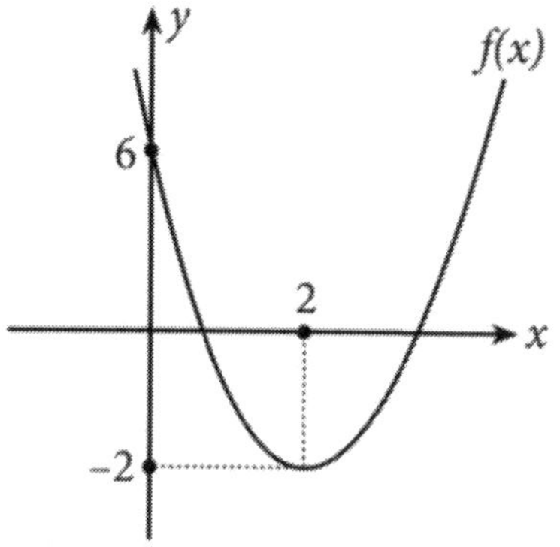

The parabola of $f(x)$ is drawn above. What is the value of $f(-1)$?

A) 7

B) 16

C) 18

D) 20

65

$$(x - 5)^2 - x + 5 - 12 = 0$$

What is the sum of the values of x that satisfy the equation given above?

A) 1
B) 2
C) 9
D) 11

66

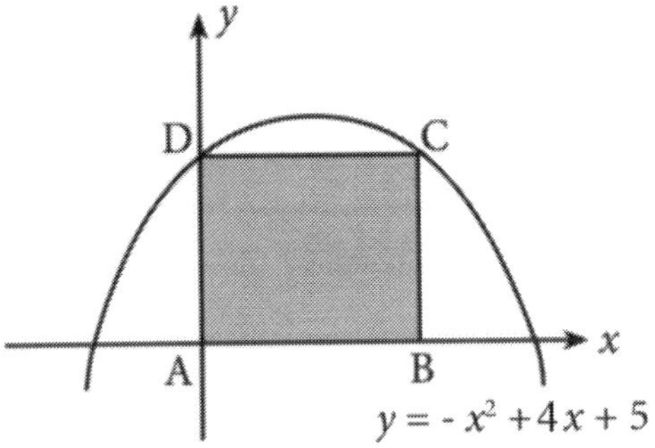

Given the graph and formula of the parabola above, what is the area of the rectangle ABCD?

A) 16
B) 20
C) 25
D) 36

67

$$(ax - 5)(bx + 2) = 12x^2 + cx - 10$$

If $ab = 12$ and $b - a = 1$, which of the following is a possible value of c?

A) -14
B) -6
C) 20
D) 26

68

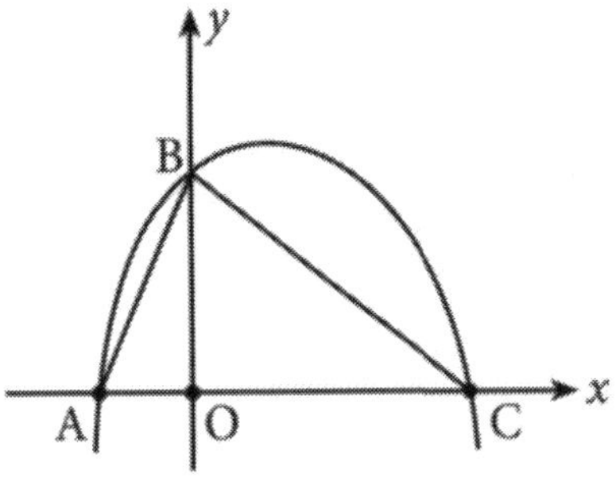

The parabola $y = -x^2 + 4x + k + 1$, and the triangle ABC are given above. If OC=3OA, what is the area of ΔABC?

A) 24
B) 36
C) 48
D) 96

CONTINUE ▶

69

As a bird descends to the ground, its distance in meters above the surface is modeled by the equation $h(t) = 0.2kt^2$.

If t is the time in seconds and it takes the bird 5 seconds to descend the final 22 meters to the surface, what is the value of the deceleration constant k?

70

If $g(x) = x^2 - 5x + 4$, what is $g(8) - g(-3)$?

71

$$y = mx^2 - 6x + n$$

If the vertex of the parabola is (-1,5), then what is the value of n?

72

$$y = 3(x + 5)^2 - 45$$

What is the y-intercept of the equation given above?

73

If $8x(x + 4) = 4x(2x + 7) + 12$, what is the value of x?

74

$$y = 2x^2 - mx + n$$

If the vertex of the parabola is (1,5), then what is the value of $m + n$?

CONTINUE ▶

75

$$y = (m^2 + 3)x^2 - 2(2m - 1)x + 5$$

If the vertex of the parabola is on the y-axis, then what is the value of m?

76

$$\sqrt{3x+12} = x+4$$

What is the product of the solutions for x in the equation above?

77

$$25x^2 + mx + 64$$

For what value of m is the equation above a perfect square?

78

$$C(x) = 0.025x^2 - 8.5x + 25{,}304$$

Steve produces phone cases in his factory. He knows the cost per phone case will decrease if he produces more. He also knows that the cost will eventually go up if he produces too many phone cases due to the overstock's storage costs. The cost of making phone cases a day is formulated above.

Find the daily production level, x, to minimize the cost.

79

$$y = mx^2 + nx + k$$

If the points (-2,5), (0,2) and (3,15) are on the parabola, what is the value of $m + n + k$?

80

$$6x - \sqrt{x} - 14 = -2 \qquad 5\sqrt{x} - 7 = A$$

Given the equations above, what is the value of A?

CONTINUE ▶

SECTION 5 - QUADRATIC EQUATIONS

#	Answer	Topic	Subtopic	#	Answer	Topic	Subtopic	#	Answer	Topic	Subtopic	#	Answer	Topic	Subtopic
1	A	TB	S1	21	C	TB	S1	41	C	TB	S1	61	A	TB	S1
2	C	TB	S1	22	A	TB	S1	42	D	TB	S1	62	D	TB	S1
3	C	TB	S1	23	B	TB	S1	43	D	TB	S1	63	C	TB	S1
4	D	TB	S1	24	D	TB	S1	44	D	TB	S1	64	B	TB	S1
5	D	TB	S1	25	B	TB	S1	45	C	TB	S1	65	D	TB	S1
6	D	TB	S1	26	D	TB	S1	46	B	TB	S1	66	B	TB	S1
7	D	TB	S1	27	D	TB	S14	47	A	TB	S1	67	A	TB	S1
8	D	TB	S1	28	B	TB	S1	48	C	TB	S1	68	C	TB	S1
9	B	TB	S1	29	B	TB	S1	49	D	TB	S1	69	4.4	TB	S1
10	C	TB	S1	30	B	TB	S1	50	D	TB	S1	70	0	TB	S1
11	D	TB	S1	31	D	TB	S1	51	B	TB	S1	71	2	TB	S1
12	D	TB	S1	32	D	TB	S1	52	C	TB	S1	72	30	TB	S1
13	A	TB	S1	33	B	TB	S1	53	D	TB	S1	73	3	TB	S1
14	A	TB	S1	34	C	TB	S1	54	C	TB	S1	74	11	TB	S1
15	C	TB	S1	35	C	TB	S1	55	D	TB	S1	75	0.5	TB	S1
16	B	TB	S1	36	C	TB	S1	56	A	TB	S1	76	4	TB	S1
17	D	TB	S1	37	D	TB	S1	57	A	TB	S1	77	80	TB	S1
18	D	TB	S1	38	C	TB	S1	58	A	TB	S1	78	170	TB	S1
19	C	TB	S1	39	B	TB	S1	59	B	TB	S1	79	4	TB	S1
20	A	TB	S1	40	C	TB	S1	60	C	TB	S1	80	0.5	TB	S1

Topics & Subtopics

Code	Description
SB1	Quadratic Equations
SB14	Functions

Code	Description
TB	Passport to Advanced Mathematics

CONTINUE ▶

1

$$K(x) = x^2 - 4x - 5$$

When $K(x)$ is shifted 2 units right and reflected over the y-axis, you get $M(x)$.

If the area bounded by the parabola $K(x)$ and the x-axis is A, then what is the area bounded by $M(x)$ and the x-axis in terms of A?

→ 2 units right

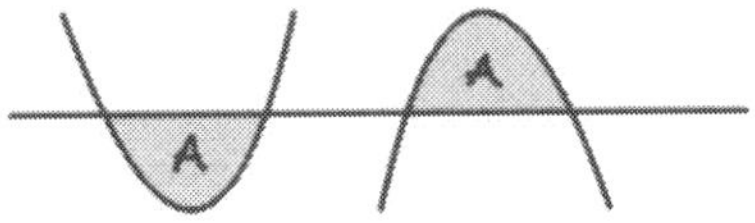

A) A
B) 2A
C) 2 + A
D) 2 - A

→ reflected over y-axis
Same area

2

$$y = -(x+3)^2 - 2$$

$y = a(x-h)^2 + k$

The graph of the equation given above in the xy-plane is a parabola. Which of the following is true about this parabola?

$(h,k) \to (-3,-2)$ vertex, max point.

A) Its minimum occurs at (3,2)
B) Its minimum occurs at (-3,2)
C) Its maximum occurs at (-3,-2)
D) Its maximum occurs at (3,-2)

3

If the vertex of a parabola is located in Quadrant I and no point in the parabola is located in Quadrant IV, which of the following must be true?

concave up $a > 0$

ax^2+bx+c

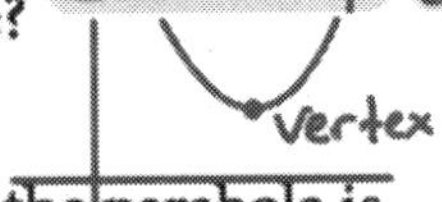

A) The x-intercept of the parabola is negative. It may also be positive.
B) The y-intercept of the parabola is negative.
C) The coefficient for the x-squared term is positive.
D) No point in the parabola is located in Quadrant III. Some points may be in QIII

4

$$y = x^2 + 6x + m$$

If the vertex of the parabola given above is 5 units away from the origin, what is the value of m?

$v\left(-\frac{b}{2a}, f\left(-\frac{b}{2a}\right)\right)$

$-\frac{b}{2a} = -\frac{6}{2 \cdot 1} = -3$

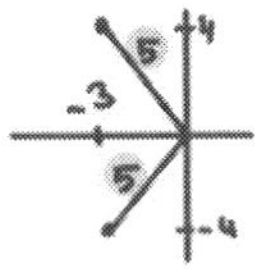

$f(-3) = (-3)^2 + 6(-3) + m = -9 + m$

$-9 + m = 4$ or $-9 + m = -4$

$m = 13$ $\quad$ $m = 5$

A) -31
B) -4
C) 4
D) 5

5

$$\sqrt{(x+4)^2} = \sqrt{36}$$

$|x+4| = 6$

Which of the following are solutions to the quadratic equation given above?

$|x+4| = 6$

$x + 4 = 6$ $\quad$ $x + 4 = -6$

$x = 2$ $\quad$ $x = -10$

A) -6 and 6
B) -5 and 4
C) -5 and 5
D) -10 and 2

6

$$y = 4(x+5)(x-7)$$

$x = -5$ $\quad$ $x = 7$

The vertex of the quadratic equation given above is (h, k). Which of the following is the value of k?

x coordinate of vertex is the midpoint of the roots $h = \frac{7-5}{2} = 1$

$y = 4(1+5)\cdot(1-7)$

$k = 4 \cdot 6 \cdot (-6) = -144$

A) -36
B) 36
C) 144
D) -144

CONTINUE ▶

7

If $(x + k)^2 = x^2 + 23x + k^2$, what is the value of k^2?

$(x+k)^2 = x^2 + 2kx + k^2$

A) 72.25

B) 90.25

C) 132.25

D) 264.50

$\dfrac{2k}{2} = \dfrac{23}{2}$　　$k = \dfrac{23}{2}$

$k^2 = \dfrac{529}{2} = 264.5$

8

$y = 2x^2 - 4x + m - 1$

$-\dfrac{b}{2a} = -\dfrac{-4}{2\cdot2} = 1$

If the minimum value of the parabola given above is 1, then what is the value of m?

$V\left(-\dfrac{b}{2a}, f\left(-\dfrac{b}{2a}\right)\right)$

A) 1

B) 2

C) 3

D) 4

$f(1) = 2\cdot(1)^2 - 4(1) + m - 1$

$1 = 2 - 4 + m - 1$

$1 = m - 3$

$+3 \quad +3$

$m = 4$

9

$v = -4t^2 - 28t + 120$

$0 = 4t^2 + 28t - 120$

A ball is thrown vertically upwards. The velocity of the ball is calculated by the equation given above, as a function of time, where v represents velocity, in meter per second and t represents time, in seconds.

How many seconds after throwing the ball the velocity of the ball become zero?

$\dfrac{4t^2 + 28t - 120}{4} = \dfrac{0}{4}$

$t^2 + 7t - 30 = 0$

$(t + 10)\cdot(t - 3) = 0$

$t = -10 \cap t = 3$

A) 2

B) 3

C) 4

D) 5

10

You are asked to construct a rectangular area with a 500m roll of fencing. What are the dimensions of the largest area?

$2x + 2y = 500$

$A(x) = x\cdot(250 - x)$

$A(x) = -x^2 + 250x$

$-\dfrac{b}{2a} = -\dfrac{250}{2(-1)} = 125$ maximum area

A) Length is 150m, width is 100m.

B) Length is 200m, width is 50m.

C) Length and width is 125m.

D) Length and width is 150m.

11

$2x^2 + 12x + c = 0$

$5x^2 + bx + 20 = 0$

If the roots of the quadratic equations given above are the same, what is the value of $c + b$?

$\dfrac{2}{5} = \dfrac{12}{b}$　　$\dfrac{2}{5} = \dfrac{c}{20}$

$\dfrac{2b}{2} = \dfrac{5\cdot12}{2}$　　$\dfrac{5c}{5} = \dfrac{2\cdot20^4}{5}$

$b = 30$　　$c = 8$

$b + c = 30 + 8 = 38$

A) 8

B) 20

C) 30

D) 38

12

$y = x^2 - mx + 5$

x-coordinate of the vertex; $-\dfrac{b}{2a}$

If the symmetry axis of the parabola given above is $x = 2$, then what is the value of m?

$1x^2 - mx + c = ax^2 + bx + c$

$-\dfrac{b}{2a} = -\dfrac{-m}{2\cdot1} = \dfrac{m}{2}$

$2 \cdot \dfrac{m}{2} = 2\cdot2$

$m = 4$

A) -2

B) -1

C) 2

D) 4

13

$$B = 2x + 10 \qquad S = x^2 - 4x + 80$$

Profit = S − B = $x^2 - 4x + 80 - (2x + 10)$

Buying price, B, and selling price, S, of a product, in dollars, is given above. What is the minimum profit, in dollars, that can be made by selling this item?

$v\left(-\frac{b}{2a}, f\left(-\frac{b}{2a}\right)\right)$ $\quad \frac{-b}{2a} = -\frac{-6}{2\cdot 1} = 3$

A) 61 $\quad P(x) = x^2 - 6x + 70$

B) 69 $\quad P(3) = 3^2 - 6\cdot 3 + 70$

C) 81 $\quad P(3) = 9 - 18 + 70$

D) 97 $\quad P(3) = 61$

14

$$3(5x^2 + 1) - 4 = 7x^2 + 3$$

$+4 \qquad +4$

same number added to both sides

When solving the equation given above, Jenna wrote $3(5x^2 + 1) = 7x^2 + 7$ as her first step. Which property justifies Jenna's first step?

A) Addition property of equality

B) Commutative property of addition

C) Multiplication property of equality

D) Distributive property of multiplication over addition

15

$$h(t) = -12t^2 + 248t$$

Willian throws a ball up in a competition in a summer camp sports activity. The above quadratic equation gives the ball's height in meter, h, as a function of time, t, in seconds.

How many meters is the height of the ball 5 seconds after it has been thrown up?

A) 52 $\quad h(5) = -12\cdot 5^2 + 248\cdot 5$

B) 300 $\quad h(5) = -12\cdot 25 + 1{,}240$

C) 940 $\quad h(5) = -300 + 1{,}240$

D) 1,240 $\quad h(5) = 940$

16

$$x - 5 = \sqrt{4x + 1}$$

What value of x is a solution for the equation given above?

Instead of solving, just try 2 and 12

~~A) 2~~ $\quad 2 - 5 \neq \sqrt{4\cdot 2 + 1}$

B) 12 $\quad 12 - 5 = \sqrt{4\cdot 12 + 1} \qquad 7 = \sqrt{49}$

~~C) 2 and 12~~

~~D) None of the above~~

CONTINUE ▶

17

$$y = x^2 + (a-3)x + 5$$
$$ax^2 + b x + c$$

If the vertex of the parabola given above is on the line of $x = -4$, what is the value of a?

$$V\left(-\frac{b}{2a}, f\left(-\frac{b}{2a}\right)\right)$$
$$\downarrow$$
$$x\text{-coordinate of vertex.}$$

A) -5

B) -1 $2 \cdot \frac{-(a-3)}{2 \cdot 1} = -4 \cdot 2$ $-(a-3) = -8$

C) 7 $a-3 = 8$

D) 11 $+3 \quad +3$

$a = 11$

18

If $(x+2)^2 = 11$, what is the value of $x^2 + 4x$?

$$x^2 + 2 \cdot 2 \cdot x + 2^2 = 11$$
$$x^2 + 4x + 4 = 11$$
$$-4 \quad -4$$

A) 4

B) 7 $x^2 + 4x = 7$

C) 9

D) 15

19

$$y = (m-3)x^2 - mx + 11$$
$$-\frac{b}{2a} = 2 \qquad ax^2 + bx + c \qquad \frac{-m}{2(m-3)} = 2$$

If the vertex of the parabola is on (2,7), what is the value of m?

$$2(m-3)\frac{m}{2(m-3)} = 2 \cdot 2(m-3) \quad m = 4(m-3)$$
$$m = 4m - 12$$
A) 2 $-4m \quad -4m$

B) 3 $\frac{-3m}{-3} = \frac{-12}{-3}$

C) 4 $m = 4$

D) 6

20

$$y = (m^2 - 16)x^2 - (2m-6)x + 12$$

If the vertex of the parabola is on the y-axis, then what is the value of m?

$$-\frac{b}{2a} = 0$$

A) 3 $-\frac{-(2m-6)}{2 \cdot (m^2-16)} = 0 \quad 2m - 6 = 0$

B) 4 $+6 \quad +6$

C) 6 $\frac{2m}{2} = \frac{6}{2}$

D) 16 $m = 3$

21

$$y = mx^2 + (m-1)x + 3$$
$$y = ax^2 + bx + c$$

If the vertex of the parabola is on the y-axis, then what is the value of m?

$$V\left(-\frac{b}{2a}, f\left(-\frac{b}{2a}\right)\right) \quad -\frac{b}{2a} = -\frac{m-1}{2m} = \frac{1-m}{2m} = 0$$

A) -1

B) 0 $2m \cdot \frac{1-m}{2m} = 0 \cdot 2m$

C) 1 $1 - m = 0 \qquad -m = -1$

D) 3 $-1 \quad -1 \qquad m = 1$

22

$$x^2 - bx + c = 0$$

One of the roots of the quadratic equation given above is -2. If the sum of the roots is 5, then what is the value of c?

$$-2 + x_2 = 5 \qquad x_2 = 7$$
$$+2 \qquad +2$$

A) -14 $(x - x_1) \cdot (x - x_2)$

B) -12 $(x - (-2)) \cdot (x - 7) = (x+2) \cdot (x-7)$

C) -10 $x^2 - 7x + 2x - 14$

D) 7

23

$$x^2+3x-4=0$$

$(x+4)\cdot(x-1)=0$ $x_1=-4$ $x_2=1$

Roots of the quadratic equation given above are m and n. Which of the following is the quadratic equation that has roots $m+2$ and $n+2$?

$-4+2=-2$

$1+2=3$

$(x-3)(x+2)$

x^2-x-6

A) x^2+5x-2

B) x^2-x-6

C) x^2+7x+6

D) x^2+7x

24

$$y=(m-3)x^2-4x+1$$

If the parabola above is tangent to the x-axis, then what is the value of m?

It has a double root; $\Delta=0$ $b^2-4ac=0$

$(-4)^2-4(m-3)\cdot1=0$

$16-4m+12=0$

$+4m$ $+4m$

$\frac{28}{4}=\frac{4m}{4}$ $m=7$

A) 3

B) 4

C) 6

D) 7

25

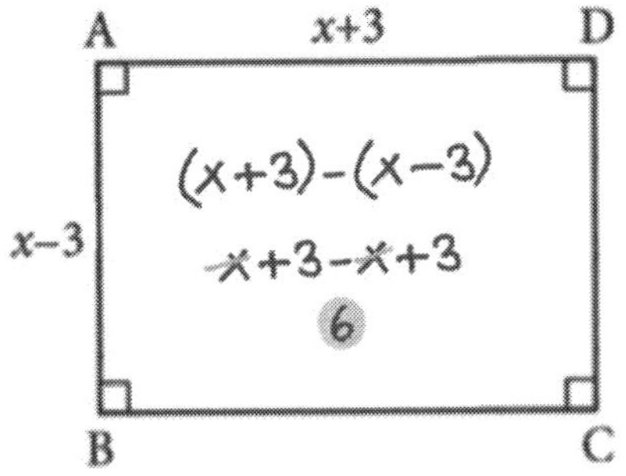

If the area of the rectangle ABCD is 36, then what is the difference in length and width?

A) 5

B) 6

C) 9

D) 16

26

$$x^2-5(x+3)=0$$

$x^2-5x-15=0$

Which of the following expressions best describe the quadratic equation above?

$\Delta=b^2-4ac=(-5)^2-4\cdot1\cdot(-15)=25+60=85>0$

A) No solution $\Delta>0$ Two real solutions

B) One real solution

C) Two imaginary solutions

D) Two real solutions

CONTINUE ▶

27

x	1	2	3	4	5	6	7
$f(x)$	7	0	-5	-8	-9	-8	-5

Use your graphing calculator;

A quadratic function of $f(x)$ is given above. What is the sum of the roots of this function?

1. Press "stat"
2. Select "edit"
3. Enter x & y values
4. Press "stat"
5. Select "CALC"
6. Select "QuadReg"
7. Select "Calculate"

L1: 1, 2, 3; L2: 7, 0, -5

$a=1$ $b=-10$ $c=16$

$ax^2+bx+c = x^2-10x+16=0$

$(x-2)\cdot(x-8)=0$ $x_1=2$ $x_2=8$

$x_1+x_2=2+8=10$

A) 2
B) 5
C) 8
D) 10

28

$$y = x^2 + 2$$
$$y = -x^2 + 4$$

$x^2+2 = -x^2+4$; $2=2x^2$; $x^2=1$

If the graphs of the parabolas given above intersect at two different points, (m,n) and (p,q), what is the value of $m + n + p + q$?

A) 0
B) 6
C) 7
D) 8

$y=1^2+2=3$ $(1,3)$

$y=(-1)^2+2=3$ $(-1,3)$

$m+n+p+q=1+3-1+3=6$

29

$$y = -4x^2 + 16x$$

$y=-4x(x-4)=0$

How many solutions does the quadratic equation given above have?

$x=0$ and $x=4$ are the roots.

A) There is no solution.
B) There are two solutions.
C) There is only one solution.
D) It can not be determined.

30

$$3x^2 + y^2 = 76$$

Based on the equation given above, which of the following is a possible value for y if both x and y are integers?

A) -5
B) -1
C) 0
D) 5

x	y	$3x^2$	y^2	$3x^2+y^2$
ӓ	-5	51	25	76
∓5	-1	75	1	76
ӓ	0	76	0	76
ӓ	5	51	25	76

31

$$y = x^2 + 6x - 16$$

$-\frac{b}{2a} = -\frac{6}{2\cdot 1} = -3$ $f(-3)=(-3)^2+6(-3)-16=-25$

Which of the following about the parabola given above is not correct?

$(x+8)(x-2)$; root are -8 and 2; -8 d=10 2

A) It has a minimum at (-3,-25). ✓
B) Distance between the roots is 10. ✓
C) Average of the roots is -3. ✓ $\frac{-8+2}{2}$
D) Sum of the roots is -6, and multiplication of the roots is 16.

$-8\times 2=-16$

32

If $x^2 + 2xy + y^2 = 81$ and $y - 3x = -39$, which of the following could be the value of x?

$(x+y)^2=81$ $y=3x-39$

$(x+3x-39)^2=81$

$\sqrt{(4x-39)^2}=81$ $4x-39=9$; $4x=48$; $x=12$

A) 6
B) 8
C) 10
D) 12

CONTINUE ▶

33

In which of the following quadratic equations sum of the roots is equal to the product of the roots?

$\frac{-b}{a} = \frac{c}{a}$

A) x^2+3x+2 $\quad -\frac{3}{1} \neq \frac{2}{1}$

B) x^2-3x+3 $\quad -\frac{-3}{1} = \frac{3}{1}$

C) x^2+4x-5 $\quad -\frac{4}{1} \neq \frac{-5}{1}$

D) x^2-4 $\quad -\frac{0}{1} \neq \frac{-4}{1}$

34

$$2x^2 - 5x = 3$$

$-3 \quad -3$

What value of x satisfies the equation given above?

A) -1

B) 1

C) 3

D) 4

$2x^2-5x-3=0$

$(2x+1)(x-3)=0$

$x=-\frac{1}{2}$ or $x=3$

35

$$x^2 - mx + m + 3 = 0$$

Double root $\Delta=0$ $\quad b^2-4ac=0$

If the quadratic equation above has a double root, what is the sum of the values of m?

$(-m)^2-4\cdot1\cdot(m+3)=0$

$m^2-4m-12=0$

$(m-6)(m+2)=0$

$m=6 \quad m=-2$

$6+(-2)=4$

A) -4

B) -2

C) 4

D) 6

36

Which of the following is the equation of the quadratic function whose roots are $1+\sqrt{6}$ and $1-\sqrt{6}$.

$(x-x_1)(x-x_2)=(x-(1+\sqrt{6}))\cdot(x-(1-\sqrt{6}))$

$x^2-x(1-\sqrt{6})-x(1+\sqrt{6})-(1+\sqrt{6})(1-\sqrt{6}))$

A) x^2-2x+5

B) x^2+2x-5 $\quad x^2-x+x\sqrt{6}-x-x\sqrt{6}+(1-6)$

C) x^2-2x-5 $\quad x^2-2x-5$

D) x^2-x-5

37

$$a=d^2-5d-14$$

The amount of water in a pool is calculated by the equation given above as a function of day, where *a* represents the amount of water, in tons and *d* represents time, in days.

How many days will it take for the amount of water in the pool to become zero?

$d^2-5d-14=0$

$(d-7)(d+2)=0$

$d=7 \quad d=-2$

days can NOT be -ve.

A) 2

B) 3

C) 5

D) 7

38

Compared to the graph of $y=x^2$, the graph of $y=(x-3)^2-2$ is;

3 units right 2 units down

A) Shifted 3 units right and 2 units up

B) Shifted 3 units left and 2 units down

C) Shifted 3 units right and 2 units down

D) Shifted 2 units down and 3 units down

CONTINUE ▶

39

Which of the following expression is true for the function $y = -4(x-2)^2$?

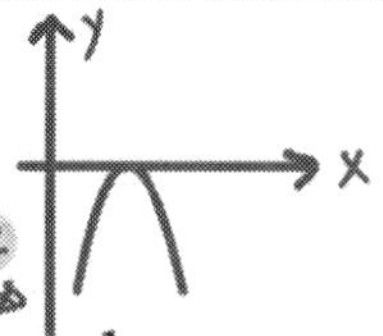

Domain: all real numbers.
Range: all -ve numbers.

A) The y-intercept is ~~16.~~ -ve

B) The range is all negative numbers.

C) The domain is all ~~positive~~ numbers.

D) The graph of the function never goes ~~below~~ the x-axis. Never above x-axis

40

$l = (x+6) \quad w = (4-x)$

$A(x) = (x+6)\cdot(4-x) = -x^2 - 2x + 24$

The length and width of a rectangle are given above. What is the maximum value for the area of this rectangle?

$v\left(-\frac{b}{2a}, f\left(-\frac{b}{2a}\right)\right) \quad -\frac{b}{2a} = -\frac{-2}{2\cdot(-1)} = -1$

A) 20

B) 24

C) 25

D) 30

$f(-1) = -(-1)^2 - 2\cdot(-1) + 24$

$f(-1) = -1 + 2 + 24 = 25$

41

In the event of a 6-day sale of the Pi Bakery, the number of cupcakes is modeled by the quadratic function $c(x) = -0.75x^2 + 1{,}323$, where x is the number of working hours from 8 am to 5 pm.

$0 = -0.75x^2 + 1{,}323 \quad 0.75x^2 = 1{,}323 \quad x^2 = 1764 \quad x = 42$

Based on this information, and assuming no intervention to change the path of the number of cupcakes, which of the following statements must be true?

$42 = 9+9+9+9+6 \qquad 8+6 = 14 = 2\text{pm}$

A) At the begining of the event there are ~~1,764~~ cupcakes. 1,323 at the begining.

B) The number of cupcakes is decreasing at a constant rate. Not a linear function

C) There will be no cupcakes left at 2 pm on Day 5 of the event.

D) The number of cupcakes will ~~increase~~ or decrease from the initial number after 8 am on the first day of the event.

42

Which of the following expression is NOT true for the function $h(x) = 3(x-4)^2$?

Domain: all real numbers.
Range: all +ve numbers.

A) The domain is all real numbers. ✓

B) The range is all positive numbers. ✓

C) The graph of the function never goes below the x-axis. Range is not -ve.

D) The graph of the function touches the x-axis where $x = -4$.

$h(-4) = 3(-4-4)^2 \neq 0$ ☹

43

$$y = (x - 4)^2$$

In the xy-plane, the parabola given above intersects the line with the equation $y = 49$ at two points, A and B. What is the length of AB?

$(x-4)^2 = 49$

A) 3 $x-4 = 7$ or $x-4 = -7$
        $+4 \quad +4$ $+4 \quad +4$
B) 9 $x = 11$ $x = -3$

C) 11   14

D) 14 $-3 \quad 0 \quad 11$

44

$$16x^2 + ax + 9$$
$$4x \qquad 3$$

What value of a makes the equation given above a perfect square?

A) 3 $(4x+3)^2 = 16x^2 + 2 \cdot 4x \cdot 3 + 3^2$

B) 4 $(4x+3)^2 = 16x^2 + 24x + 3^2$

C) 12

D) 24

45

$$(5-x) \cdot \frac{2x^2 - 3}{5-x} = -7 \cdot (5-x)$$
$$2x^2 - 3 = 7x^2 - 35$$

Which of the following statements about the equation above is true? $5x^2 - 32 = 0$
                                                                       $+32 \quad +32$
$2x^2 - 3 = 7x^2 - 35$ $\frac{5x^2}{5} = \frac{32}{5} \quad x^2 = \frac{32}{5}$
$-2x^2 +3 \quad -2x^2 +3$

A) The equation has no solutions. $x = \mp\sqrt{\frac{32}{5}}$

B) The equation has exactly one solution.

C) The equation has exactly two solutions.

D) The equation has infinitely many solutions.

46

$$P(x) = ax^2 + bx + c$$

Given the quadratic equation above, what is the value of $a + c$, if $P(1) = 10$ and $P(-1) = 6$?

$P(1) = a(1)^2 + b(1) + c = 10$
$a + b + c = 10$
A) 6 $P(-1) = a(-1)^2 + b(-1) + c = 6$
B) 8 $a - b + c = 6$
C) 10 $a + b + c = 10$
         $+ a - b + c = 6$
D) 16 $\frac{2(a+c)}{2} = \frac{16}{2}$ $a+c = 8$

47

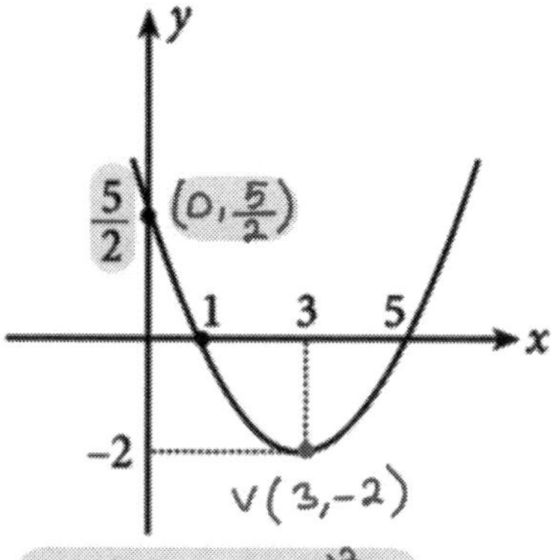

$f(x) = a(x-3)^2 - 2$

Which of the following represents the parabola shown above?

A) $f(x) = \frac{1}{2}(x-3)^2 - 2$

B) $f(x) = \frac{1}{2}(x+3)^2 + \frac{5}{2}$

C) $f(x) = (x-3)^2 + \frac{5}{2}$

D) $f(x) = (x+2)^2 + 3$

48

$$1x^2 + 2x + 2 = 0$$

$$ax^2 + bx + c$$

Which of the following is a solution to the quadratic equation given above?

$\frac{-b \mp \sqrt{b^2 - 4ac}}{2a} = \frac{-2 \mp \sqrt{2^2 - 4 \cdot 1 \cdot 2}}{2 \cdot 1} = \frac{-2 \mp \sqrt{4-8}}{2} = \frac{-2 \mp \sqrt{-4}}{2} = \frac{-2 \mp 2i}{2} = -1 \mp i$

A) 1 - 2i

B) 1 + 2i

C) -1 - i

D) - i

49

$$y = mx^2 + (m-1)x + 2m - 1$$

If the parabola given above passes through the point (2,9), what is the value of m?

$y(2) = m \cdot 2^2 + (m-1)2 + 2m - 1$

$9 = 4m + 2m - 2 + 2m - 1$

$9 = 8m - 3$

$\frac{12}{8} = \frac{8m}{8}$ $m = 1.5$

A) 0.66

B) 0.75

C) 1.33

D) 1.50

50

$$x^2 + ax + b = 0$$

$x_1 + x_2 = -\frac{a}{1} = -a$ negative

In the quadratic equation above $b < 0 < a$. Which of the following about the roots of this quadratic equation is true?

$x_1 + x_2 = \frac{-b + \sqrt{\Delta}}{2a} + \frac{-b - \sqrt{\Delta}}{2a} = \frac{-2b}{2a} = \frac{-b}{a}$

A) It does not have real roots.

B) The roots are equal.

C) It has two positive roots.

D) The sum of the roots is negative. ✓

51

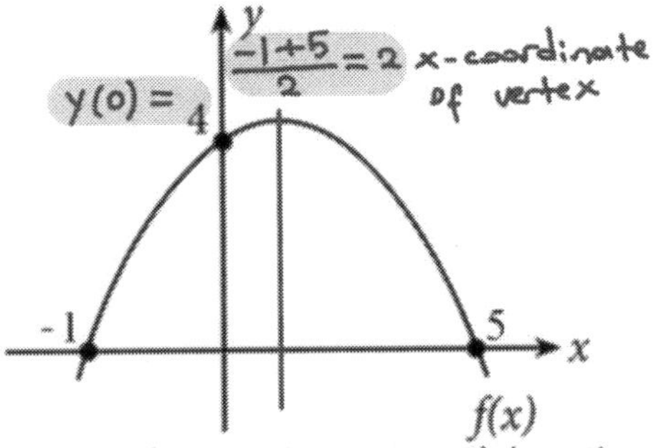

$y = a(x-(-1))(x-5) = a(x+1)(x-5)$

The parabola of $f(x) = ax^2 + bx + c$ is given above. What is the value of a?

A) -0.40
B) -0.80
C) -1.25
D) 4

$y(0) = a(0+1)(0-5)$

$\frac{4}{-5} = \frac{-5a}{-5}$ $a = -0.8$

52

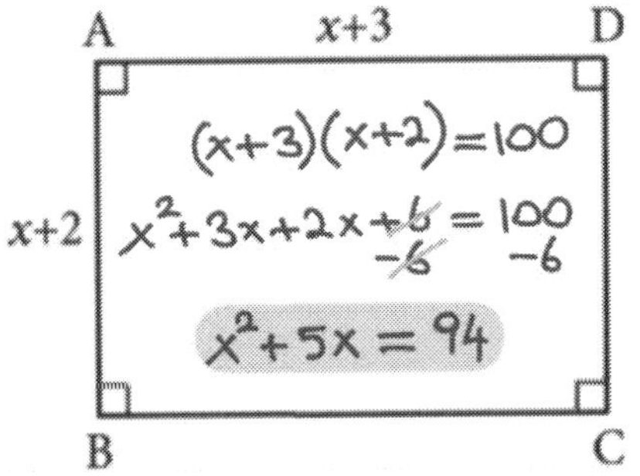

Area of the rectangle above is 100. What is the area of a square whose side is $2x + 5$?

A) 119
B) 400
C) 401
D) 449

$(2x+5)^2 = (2x)^2 + 2 \cdot 2x \cdot 5 + 5^2$
$= 4x^2 + 20x + 25$
$= 4(x^2 + 5x) + 25$
$= 4 \cdot 94 + 25$
$= 401$

53

$$x^2 + 13x + 36 = (x + a)(x + b)$$

In the quadratic equation given above, b is an integer. Which of the following is a possible value of b? $a \cdot b = 36$ $a + b = 13$

	a	b	$a \cdot b$	$a+b$
A) 3	12	3	36	15
B) 5	×	5	36	
C) 7	×	7	36	
D) 9	4	9	36	13

54

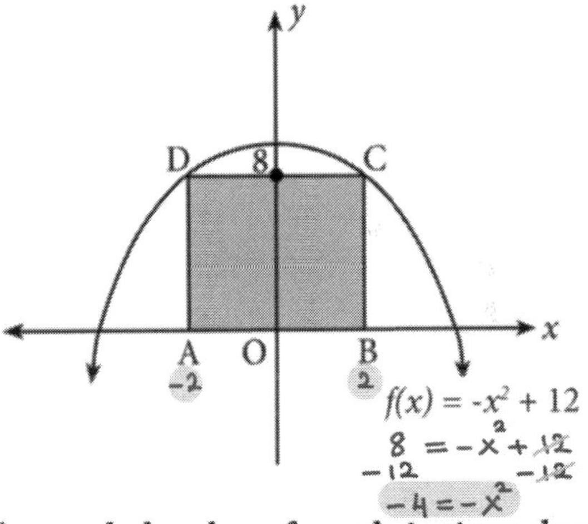

The parabola, whose formula is given above, intersects with two corners of the rectangle ABCD. What is the area of the rectangle ABCD? $x^2 = 4$ $x = 2, -2$

A) 8
B) 16
C) 32
D) 48

8 $8 \cdot 4 = 32$ 4

55

If the points (-1,3), (0,2) and (2,12) are on the parabola $y = ax^2 + bx + c$, what is the value of $a + b + c$? Use your graphing calculator;

1. Press "stat"
2. Select "edit"
3. Enter x & y values
4. Press "stat"
5. Select "CALC"
6. Select "QuadReg"
7. Select "Calculate"

L1	L2
-1	3
0	2
2	12

$a=2$ $b=1$ $c=2$

$a+b+c=2+1+2=5$

A) 1
B) 2
C) 3
D) 5

56

$$f(x) = A(x-8)(x+2)$$

roots; $x=8$ $x=-2$

In the quadratic function given above, A is a non-zero constant. The graph of the function in the *xy* plane has a vertex at the point (h,k). Which of the following is the value of k?

x coordinate of vertex is the midpoint of the roots $h=\frac{8-2}{2}=3$

$f(3) = A(3-8)\cdot(3+2)$

$k = A\cdot(-5)\cdot 5 = -25A$

A) -25A
B) -16A
C) 11A
D) 64A

57

K: $-3x^2+x+4$ M: $3x^2-x+4$

~~L~~: $-3x^2+x-4$ ~~N~~: $3x^2-x-4$

$L(0)=-4\neq 4$ $N(0)=-4\neq 4$

Which one is the equation of the parabola that passes through the points A(-1,0), B(0,4), and C(1,2)? Using B(0,4) you eliminate L & N

Test (-1,0);

A) K $K(-1)=-3(-1)^2+(-1)+4$
B) L $K(-1)=-3-1+4=0$ ✓
C) M $M(-1)=3(-1)^2-(-1)+4$
D) N $M(-1)=3+1+4=8$

58

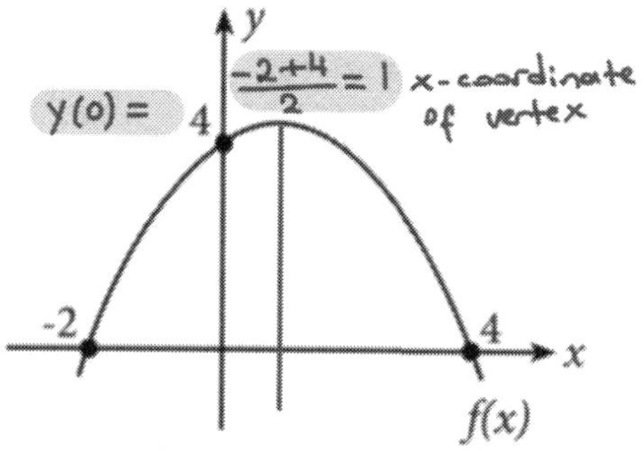

$y=a(x-(-2))(x-4)=a(x+2)(x-4)$

The parabola of $f(x)$ is given above. What is the maximum value of $f(x)$?

$y(0)=a(0+2)(0-4)$

$\frac{4}{-8}=\frac{-8a}{-8}$ $a=-0.5$

$y=-0.5(x+2)(x-4)$

$y(1)=-0.5(1+2)(1-4)$

$y(1)=-0.5\cdot 3\cdot -3=4.5$

A) 4.5
B) 5
C) 5.5
D) 6

59

$$y = x^2 - (m+3)x + m + 2$$

$4 = (-1)^2 - (m+3)(-1) + m + 2$

If the point (-1,4) is on the parabola given above, what is the distance between the origin (0,0) and the vertex of this parabola?

$4 = 1 + m + 3 + m + 2$ $\quad 4 = 2m + 6$ $\quad -6 \quad -6$ $\quad \frac{-2}{2} = \frac{2m}{2}$

$y = x^2 - (-1+3)x - 1 + 2 = x^2 - 2x + 1$ $\quad m = -1$

$v\left(-\frac{b}{2a}, f\left(-\frac{b}{2a}\right)\right)$ $\quad -\frac{b}{2a} = -\frac{-2}{2\cdot 1} = 1$

$v(1, f(1))$ $\quad f(1) = 1^2 - 2\cdot 1 + 1 = 0$

$v(1,0)$

distance=1 (0,0) (1,0)

A) 0
B) 1
C) 1.4
D) 2.4

60

$$y = x^2 + mx + n$$

$ax^2 + bx + c$

$-\frac{b}{2a} = 1$ $\quad -\frac{m}{2\cdot 1} = 1$

If the vertex of the parabola given above is at point (1,2), then what is the value of $m + n$?

$2 \cdot \frac{-m}{2\cdot 1} = 1 \cdot 2$ $\quad -m = 2$ $\quad m = -2$

$y(1) = 1^2 - 2\cdot 1 + n$

$2 = 1 - 2 + n$

$2 = -1 + n$

$+1 \quad +1$

$n = 3$ $\quad m + n = -2 + 3$ $\quad m + n = 1$

A) -1
B) 0
C) 1
D) 3

61

If the vertex of the parabola $y = ax^2 + bx + 5$ is (1,3) then what is the value of $a + b$?

$y(1) = a\cdot 1^2 + b\cdot 1 + 5$

$3 = a + b + 5$

$-5 \quad -5$

$-2 = a + b$

A) -2
B) 3
C) 5
D) 8

62

$$1\cdot x^2 + (m-1)x + 1 = 0$$

$ax^2 + bx + c$

$a=1 \quad b=m-1 \quad c=1$

The roots of the quadratic equation given above are a and b. If $ab + a + b = -10$, then what is the value of m? $\quad x_1 \cdot x_2 = \frac{c}{a}$

$x_1 + x_2 = \frac{-b+\sqrt{\Delta}}{2a} + \frac{-b-\sqrt{\Delta}}{2a} = \frac{-2b}{2a} = -\frac{b}{a}$

$ab + (a+b) = x_1 \cdot x_2 + x_1 + x_2 = -10$

$= \frac{1}{1} + \frac{-(m-1)}{1} = -10$

$1 - m + 1 = -10$

$2 - m = -10$

$-2 \quad -2$

$-m = -12$

$m = 12$

A) -12
B) -10
C) 3
D) 12

63

$$9^x - 10\cdot 3^x + 9 = 0$$

$(3^x)^2 - 10\cdot 3^x + 9$

What is the sum of the roots of the equation given above?

Let $3^x = m$

$m^2 - 10m + 9 = 0$

$(m-9)(m-1) = 0$

$m = 9 \quad m = 1$

$3^x = 3^2 \quad 3^x = 3^0$

$x = 2 \quad x = 0$

$2 + 0 = 2$

A) 0
B) 1
C) 2
D) 3

64

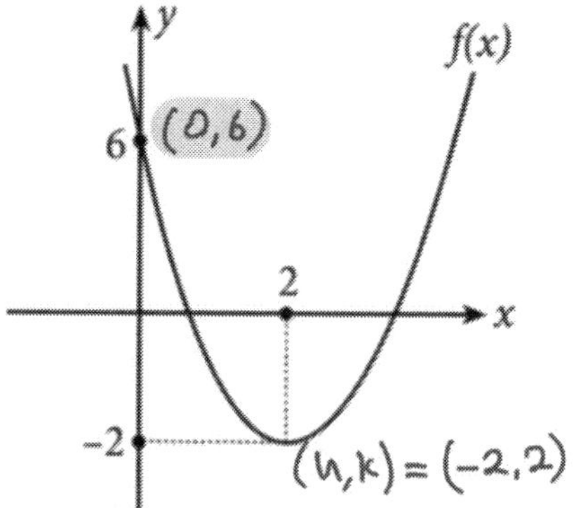

$y=a(x-h)^2+k$ $y=a(x-2)^2-2$

The parabola of $f(x)$ is drawn above. What is the value of $f(-1)$?

$6=a(0-2)^2-2$, $+2$ $+2$, $\frac{8}{4}=\frac{4a}{4}$, $a=2$

$y=2(-1-2)^2-2$, $y=2(3)^2-2$, $y=2(3)^2-2$, $y=2\cdot 9-2=16$

A) 7
B) 16
C) 18
D) 20

65

$$(x - 5)^2 - x + 5 - 12 = 0$$

Let $m=x-5$ $m^2-m-12=(m-4)(m+3)=0$

What is the sum of the values of x that satisfy the equation given above?

$m=4$: $4=x-5$, $+5$ $+5$, $x=9$

$m=-3$: $-3=x-5$, $+5$ $+5$, $x=2$

$9+2=11$

A) 1
B) 2
C) 9
D) 11

66

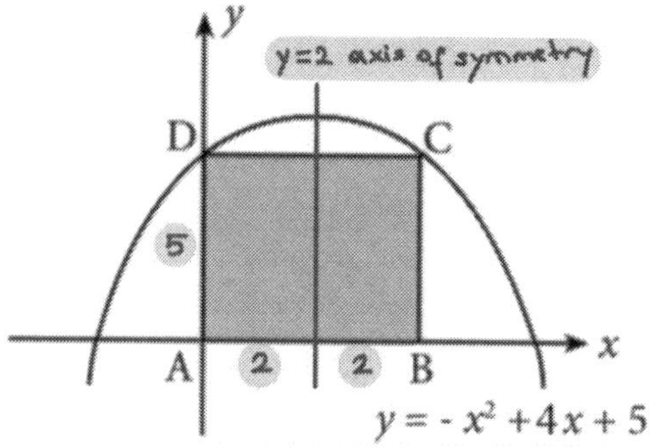

$y = -x^2 + 4x + 5$

$y(0)=-0^2+4\cdot 0+5=5$

Given the graph and formula of the parabola above, what is the area of the rectangle ABCD?

$-x^2+4x+5=0$

$-\frac{b}{2a}=-\frac{4}{2\cdot(-1)}=\frac{-4}{-2}=2$

$A=5\cdot 4$, $A=20$

A) 16
B) 20
C) 25
D) 36

67

$$(ax - 5)(bx + 2) = 12x^2 + cx - 10$$

$abx^2+2ax-5bx-10 = abx^2+(2a-5b)x-10$

If $ab = 12$ and $b - a = 1$, which of the following is a possible value of c?

$b-a=1$, $+a$ $+a$, $b=a+1$

$c=2a-5b$, $c=2a-5(a+1)$, $c=-3a-5$, $+5$ $+5$, $c+5=-3a$

c+5 must be divisible by 3.

$-14+5=-9$ is divisible by 3.

A) -14
B) -6
C) 20
D) 26

68

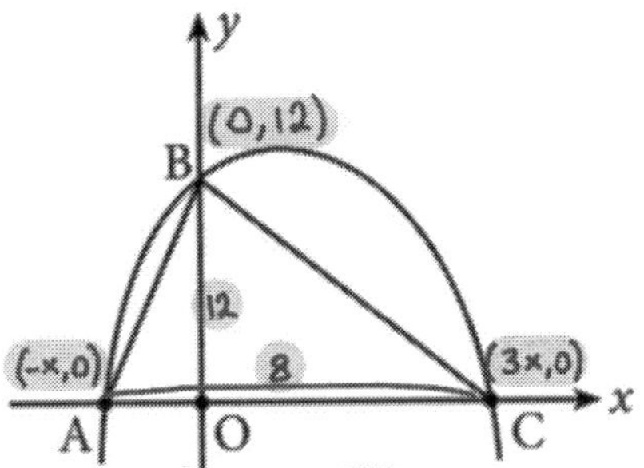

$x_1+x_2=\frac{-b+\sqrt{\Delta}}{2a}+\frac{-b-\sqrt{\Delta}}{2a}=\frac{-2b}{2a}=\frac{-b}{a}$

The parabola $y = -x^2 + 4x + k + 1$, and the triangle ABC are given above. If OC=3OA, what is the area of ΔABC?

$x_1+x_2=\frac{-b}{a}$ $y(-2)=-(-2)^2+4(-2)+k+1$

$-x+3x=-\frac{4}{-1}$ $0=-4-8+k+1$

$\frac{2x}{2}=\frac{4}{2}$ $0=-11+k$ $+11$ $+11$ $k=11$

$x=2$ $y(0)=11+1=12$

$A=\frac{1}{2}\cdot 8\cdot 12=48$

A) 24

B) 36

C) 48

D) 96

69

As a bird descends to the ground, its distance in meters above the surface is modeled by the equation $h(t) = 0.2kt^2$.

$22=0.2k(5)^2$

If t is the time in seconds and it takes the bird 5 seconds to descend the final 22 meters to the surface, what is the value of the deceleration constant k?

$22=0.2k\cdot 25$ $\frac{22}{5}=\frac{5k}{5}$ $k=4.4$

70

If $g(x) = x^2 - 5x + 4$, what is $g(8) - g(-3)$?

$g(8)=8^2-5\cdot 8+4=64-40+4=28$

$g(3)=(-3)^2-5(-3)+4=9+15+4=28$

$g(8)-g(3)=28-28=0$

71

$$y = mx^2 - 6x + n$$

If the vertex of the parabola is (-1,5), then what is the value of n?

$-\frac{b}{2a}=-1$ $-\frac{-6}{2m}=-1$ $2m\frac{6}{2m}=-1\cdot 2m$ $\frac{6}{-2}=\frac{-2m}{-2}$ $m=-3$

$5=-3(-1)^2-6(-1)+n$

$5=-3+6+n$

$5=3+n$

-3 -3

$n=2$

CONTINUE ▶

72

$y = 3(x + 5)^2 - 45$

Set x=0 and solve for y

What is the *y*-intercept of the equation given above?

$y=3(0+5)^2-45=3\cdot25-45=75-45=30$

73

If $8x(x + 4) = 4x(2x + 7) + 12$, what is the value of x?

$8x^2+32x=8x^2+28x+12$
$-28x \quad -28x$
$\frac{4x}{4}=\frac{12}{4}$ $x=3$

74

$y=2x^2-mx+n$

$v\left(-\frac{b}{2a}, f\left(-\frac{b}{2a}\right)\right)$

If the vertex of the parabola is (1,5), then what is the value of $m + n$?

$-\frac{b}{2a}=-\frac{-m}{2\cdot2}=\frac{m}{4}=1$ $m=4$

$2\cdot1^2-4\cdot1+n=5$
$-2+n=5$
$+2 \quad +2$
$n=7$

$m+n=4+7=11$

75

$y=(m^2+3)x^2-2(2m-1)x+5$

x-coordinate of the vertex is zero. $-\frac{b}{2a}=0$

If the vertex of the parabola is on the *y*-axis, then what is the value of *m*?

$2(m^2+3)\cdot -\frac{-2(2m-1)}{2\cdot(m^2+3)}=0\cdot2(m^2+3)$ $4m-2=0$
$+2 \quad +2$

$\frac{4m}{4}=\frac{2}{4}$ $m=0.5$

76

$\left(\sqrt{3x+12}\right)^2=(x+4)^2$

What is the product of the solutions for x in the equation above?

$3x+12=x^2+8x+16$
$-3x-12 \quad -3x-12$

$x^2+5x+4=0$
$(x+4)(x+1)=0$
$x=-4$ $x=-1$
$(-4)\cdot(-1)=4$

77

$25x^2+mx+64$
$5x \quad 8$

For what value of *m* is the equation above a perfect square?

$(5x+8)^2=25x^2+2\cdot5x\cdot8+64$ $m=2\cdot5\cdot8=80$

78

$$C(x) = 0.025x^2 - 8.5x + 25,304$$

$ax^2 + bx + c$

Steve produces phone cases in his factory. He knows the cost per phone case will decrease if he produces more. He also knows that the cost will eventually go up if he produces too many phone cases due to the overstock's storage costs. The cost of making phone cases a day is formulated above.

$-\frac{b}{2a} = -\frac{-8.5}{2 \cdot 0.025} = \frac{8.5}{0.05} = 170$ (min)

Find the daily production level, *x*, to minimize the cost.

79

$$y = mx^2 + nx + k$$

If the points (-2,5), (0,2) and (3,15) are on the parabola, what is the value of *m* + *n* + *k*?

Use your graphing calculator;

1. Press "stat"
2. Select "edit"
3. Enter x & y values

L1	L2
-2	5
0	2
3	15

4. Press "stat"
5. Select "CALC"
6. Select "QuadReg"
7. Select "Calculate"

$m = 1.17$ $n = 0.83$ $k = 2$

$m + n + k = 1.17 + 0.83 + 2 = 4$

80

$$6x - \sqrt{x} - 14 = -2 \qquad 5\sqrt{x} - 7 = A$$

$+2 \quad +2$

Given the equations above, what is the value of *A*? $6x - \sqrt{x} - 12 = 0$ Let $\sqrt{x} = m$ then; $x = m^2$

$6m^2 - m - 12 = 0$

$(3m+4)(2m-3) = 0$

$3m + 4 = 0$, $-4 \; -4$, $\frac{3m}{3} = \frac{-4}{3}$, $m = -\frac{4}{3}$

$2m - 3 = 0$, $+3 \; +3$, $\frac{2m}{2} = \frac{3}{2}$

$\sqrt{x}$ can not be negative

$m = 1.5 = \sqrt{x}$

$A = 5\sqrt{x} - 7 = 5 \cdot (1.5) - 7 = 7.5 - 7 = 0.5$

CONTINUE ▶

Made in the USA
Columbia, SC
20 July 2023

20667109R00083